Behi Laughter, Hidden Tears

Sal Richards

 Strategic Book Publishing

Strategic Book Publishing
An imprint of Strategic Book Group
P.O. Box 333
Durham CT 06422
www.StrategicBookGroup.com

ISBN: 978-1-60911-255-4

Printed in the United States of America

This book is dedicated to my beautiful wife, RoseAnn,

who stood with me through the good and the bad times.

Her unselfish love and courage helped me get to where

I am today.

And to my son, Guy, who conquered all his demons

and became the son who was missing for a long time.

I love you both very much.

And to my dear son, Sal Junior, whom I miss and love

every day of my life.

Contents

Foreword

Steve Schirripa

Sal Richards is a comic, singer, actor, producer, husband, and father. Most of you have heard of Sal, but probably have never met him. He has been entertaining audiences for more than fifty years in all parts of the country. I've had the pleasure of knowing Sal and working with him for about fifteen years. When you know someone in the business you may know them for a while, but you don't really "know" them, if you know what I mean…

I knew Sal had some very tough personal problems involving his family, but until I read his book I had no idea what it entailed.

This book is so much more than an entertainer telling his life's ups and downs, which we've all heard and read many times before. Behind the Laughter, Hidden Tears is a story about not just a man, but a good man who, while making many mistakes of his own doing and experiencing some horrible personal tragedies, picked himself up time and time again and became the man he is today. What Sal has endured would have caused many of us to curl up into a ball and give up, but not Sal. Over and over, hardship after hardship, he has come back stronger than ever.

This is not just a book about the "showbiz" life; it is so much more.

It's about a man who has truly done it his way. Sal lets it all hang out. This story is a true inspiration that everyone should read, not just those involved in the "showbiz" life, but for all those who have experienced problems throughout their lives and found themselves asking, "Why me?"

Something that can honestly be said about Sal is that he takes no crap from anyone, yet he is still a real gentleman. In the phony world of showbiz Sal is a breath of fresh air. This story is funny, sad, tragic, and inspiring. So sit back, pour yourself a glass of wine, and enjoy!

Salud to Sal Richards!

Prologue

I'm sitting in a waiting area at LAX Airport. I got here at 10:00 p.m. to catch a redeye back to New York. My flight was scheduled for 11:45, so I had plenty of time, right? Wrong. When I got here, I waited forty minutes at the outside baggage check-in, and by the time I got to the skycap, he said, "You're too late to check bags for this flight."

"WHAT? Hold it," I said. I was steamed. "I was here in plenty of time. You left the counter for fifteen minutes, and all the passengers were wondering where you were. Then you come back and tell me *this?*"

He didn't care what anyone had to say, so now I have to wait for the next flight—7:30 in the morning. So how do I kill over eight hours? All of sudden I think, *Well, why don't I write a book?* Then I think, *but what the hell would I write about?* Okay, so how about when my dad was killed in the Philippines, or how I fell out of a two-story building when I was five? What about how I met RoseAnn? That would be fun. Or what about my life in show business-meeting Sinatra, Dean Martin, and all the celebrities I became friends with over the years? Or maybe when I fought in the Golden Gloves, or was broke, or when my wife and I lost our firstborn after six days? Do I mention that our young son, Sal Junior, beat leukemia, only to die because of a bad reaction to some cold medications?

Well, how about if I just start at the beginning?

1

My Life Begins

February 8, 1939, happened to be a snowy day in Brooklyn. My mother, Josephine Giovia, went into labor at about 12:30 A.M., and by 2:00 A.M. I was born—me, Salvatore Giovia. It all went smooth, from what I hear. I don't know if my father was there or not—I was too young to know what was going on around me. From what I've been told, things progressed pretty well from that day forward with not too much exciting going on—up until a particular moment, which I'm about to get to.

I was in our living room, which was the end room of a railroad apartment. (Rooms in a railroad apartment, as the name implies, are in a line front to back, like the cars of a train.) World War II was going on and my father, John J. Giovia, was in the army fighting for his country in the Philippines. My mother was in the kitchen, cooking the evening meal, and my cousin Joe was watching me. I had a toy tin gun and had climbed up on the windowsill of an open window. My cousin was reading a racing form. He was known as Joe the Pony, and all he did was play the horses.

As I stood on the windowsill, I saw trolley cars coming down the street. Playing cowboy, I leaned out the window to take aim at one of the trolleys. I slipped and fell two stories to the concrete below, missing an iron gate by inches. As I sat crying in pain, an old man saw me and thought I'd fallen off the gate. As my mother told me years later, she'd walked into the end room to call us for dinner. When she asked

Joe where I was, he said, "He's, ah…I don't know." Mom looked out the window and saw me on the ground. She let out a scream and ran as fast as she could down the stairs. Just as the old man was placing me on the stoop, my mother got there and picked me up, and saw the blood gushing from my head. It was too late to call for help, Mom thought, so she hailed a cab. Two refused to stop when they saw the blood, but finally one did. Full of concern, my mother explained what had happened and said, "I'll clean up the cab later."

"Not important," the cabby said, and he took us to Wyckoff Heights Hospital. I was treated, sewn up, and sent home. My mother's quick action saved my life that day.

Months later, I was healed up and able to go to day school at the Salvation Army while my mother worked at Woolworth's Department Store and my father continued his tour with the army. Months went by, and before I knew it, it was 1945 and I was six years old. I asked Mom, "When is Daddy coming home?"

"He'll be home soon, Sal," she told me.

But that turned out not to be true. It was one of those early days that is etched in my memory, when we got the telegram informing us that my father, PFC John J. Giovia, was killed in action. It was followed by a letter from a chaplain telling us he died a hero, having saved some men from enemy fire. The worst part was, the war ended two weeks after he was killed.

My mother was devastated. I understood most of what was going on, but my brother, Joseph, was two-and-a-half years younger than me, so it didn't register with him. It was only later, when he was about seven, that he too understood.

So here we were my mom, Joey, and me—alone. My mother was a strong woman, even for her young age, and did as so many other war widows did, she took on the task of being a single mom before it was fashionable—working, getting us to school, loving us, and trying to make us happy. Thanks, Mom!

2

We Are Moving

Okay, so now things were settling down a little, and my mother decided we were going to move. So move we did, right across the street from where we lived—only this time, Mom wanted to live in a bottom-floor apartment. You can guess why. If I decided to "shoot" any more trolley cars from the window, I wouldn't have far to fall. We stayed in this new apartment until I got a little older.

Some of the famous people that were brought up in Ridgewood/Bushwick section of Brooklyn are Jackie Gleason, Julius LaRosa, Connie Stevens, Eddie Murphy, and Rosie Perez. I am proud to be among this great list of performers.

I think I was about eight when we moved again, this time to 227 Stanhope Street, Ridgewood 27, Brooklyn—which, for some reason, is now called Ridgewood, Queens. We didn't realize how that move would change our lives forever. On Saturdays we had a ritual. My mother would take us to the park to play all day while she sat and watched us. Little did she know that someone was watching and admiring her, and after a few weeks passed a man approached her and they had a conversation. She told him she was a widow with two boys and she'd lost her husband in the war, and so on.

Before long she decided it was time to go on a date with him. She did just that, and she continued seeing him. She kept it private for a while, not telling even us about him, but one day, as we were looking out of the window in the front room facing Stanhope Street, we saw a man in what we thought was a uniform of some kind walking by. Mom waved at him ever so discretely, and he waved back. That's when I noticed the gleam in her eyes and her beautiful smile.

I looked up as he went out of sight down the street and asked Mom, "Who was that man?" She explained to us that he was the "park man"—the one who worked in the park where she took us every Saturday. They'd been dating, she told us, and we finally got to know him. He was a true gentleman, and even though I was young, I could see how he cared for Mom, which wasn't hard—she was beautiful and had a great sense of humor.

Before I knew it, I was at my mother's wedding mass at St. Barbara's Church on Evergreen Avenue. *What's going on?* I thought to myself. *I think I'm getting a new daddy*—and sure enough, here we were, a family again. This man took my mother and her two sons and made us a new family. Although he never legally adopted us, he always considered us his own, never treating us as stepchildren.

He loved my mother so much that he accepted everything that went with their marriage. When the army finally sent my real father's remains home for burial at Pinelawn Soldiers Cemetery out on Long Island, my new dad took us to the ceremony. When they rolled out the casket, he said to all of us, "Go and pay your respects to your father." As we walked over to the casket, we wondered if Daddy was really in there. Of course there were a lot of tears, but the tears really flowed when my new dad took Mom by the arm and walked her to the casket for her final goodbye. She started crying hysterically, and he showed his own great emotion with tears in his eyes too. What a classy guy! Thanks, "Daddy" Stephen Massaro.

3

The Family Grows

By now my new father was working two jobs, my mother was pregnant, and the family was shaping up pretty well. I was ten, Joey was seven-and-a-half, and both of us were going to PS 86, on Irving Avenue. Life was pretty normal, the usual family life with the struggles, but going on nicely. Then, in 1950, Dad got what he needed—his own son, Stephen Junior. Boy, how happy everyone was for him and my mother when Stephen Junior was born. And I'll say this—it never changed his way of thinking. He treated us all equally.

So Dad was working, Mom was taking care of her new son, and Joey and I were going to school—a typical family starting to grow. Dad now had a job with a company called No-Sag Springs. In 1951, the company moved to Indiana, so rather than look for another job; he and Mom decided it would be beneficial to go to Indiana with the company. They kept the apartment on Stanhope Street, just in case. It was only $27 a month, so what the hell—they figured they might as well keep it.

The drive to Indiana was boring as hell, so I'll skip that part. My Aunt Mary and Uncle Phil were already there, because Uncle Phil also worked at No-Sag, and they'd gone out to set up early. Aunt Mary was my mother's sister, smaller in stature, very pleasant and loving. They got us a place to rent in Wolcottville, on the same property their house was on. *What the hell is this?* I thought when I saw it—a small cabin on Adams Lake, with one bedroom, a kitchen, and a large living room with a pull-out bed for me and Joey, and a daybed for Steven. What—no bathroom? I'd never seen anything like it in my life. The "bathroom" was outside the house, about ten yards away, and it wasn't a bathroom at all—just a wooden cubicle with a toilet seat and a big hole dug under it.

So there I was, almost twelve years old, trying to get used to an environment I never knew existed. I now had to shit and piss outside, in a small cubicle that stunk to holy hell—and when it was dark and you were sitting there and hearing the strange sounds of unknown animals, if you didn't have to go, the sounds and the dark would scare the shit out of you. And when *winter* set in, walking through three feet of snow to get to the outhouse was ridiculous. Mom solved that by going to the local general store to buy potties for everyone.

We were enrolled in the local school, and the bus came every morning at seven to pick us up. Wow—another unforeseeable thing, taking a bus to school. And there I was, a kid from Brooklyn going to school with people dressed like the picture of the guy on the oatmeal box. I found out later they were called Quakers, dressed in overalls, straw hats, boots, etc. Man, was I in the *Twilight Zone,* or what?

I celebrated my twelfth birthday on a freezing day in Indiana, surrounded by my two cousins from next door, my two brothers, Mom and Dad, and Aunt Mary and Uncle Phil. It was a great party, except for the food. See, we couldn't get the right ingredients for the Italian sauce Mom used to make—and many other dishes we were used to eating. Well, what do you expect—we're Italian, so give me a break.

Living there was quite an experience, and it made me realize just how easy life had been in Brooklyn. After seeing this alternate way of life—farmers collecting the corn, mowing the hay, taking eggs to the markets—I couldn't wait to get back to my roots, where there were no square dances, no Quakers, no outhouses, and no potties. Thankfully, Mom finally got fed up with all of it too. "Let's get out of here," she said, and back to Brooklyn we went.

4

Hello Brooklyn, Goodbye Brooklyn, Hello Centereach

Back in Brooklyn—hooray!—and back to a real school with some tough kids, pretty girls, and school dances. I was now fourteen, getting ready to graduate Junior High School 162, and that's what I did. It was mid-1953, and I was on my way to Boys High School on Marcy Avenue—in Brooklyn, of course.

I entered high school in September 1953, but I only went there for two semesters. Then I heard we were going to move again, this time out to Long Island. Mom and Dad bought a house in Centereach, in Suffolk County, so here I was, once again getting ready for culture shock.

In 1955, we moved to a cute Cape Cod on Stanley Drive, and this time Aunt Katie and Uncle Louis bought a house right next door. This family was a close one. Aunt Katie was Mom's other sister, older by a few years, and Uncle Louie was a gem of a man—big, rotund, and jolly. Their house was the same as ours, with two bedrooms, a living room and kitchen, bathroom—plus a basement. Wow. In our eyes, it was a mansion. The lot was 100 by 150, the back yard was big, there was grass all around and nice trees, but there were *no people!* Oh no, not again! But this was the start of a new development—Dawn Estates—and it was slowly growing.

7

Okay. It was time to register for school again, and this time it was Port Jefferson High School, which was a lot closer to the Long Island Sound than Centereach. Sure enough, there was another bus to take to school. Been there, done that, so it didn't matter. So here I was, a fifteen-year-old from Brooklyn with the duck's-ass haircut, pegged pants with saddle stitches down the leg, walking head-on into real, strait-laced conservative classmates wearing white buck shoes and team sweaters with PJHS on them. When they first laid eyes on me, they must have thought someone from the movie *Blackboard Jungle* had entered the room. Needless to say, school life was a little shaky and cold for a while.

So what did yours truly, the genius, do? I tried out for the football team—you know, to get with the "in crowd" at the school? What a mistake. At my first practice, those guys trampled me like I was grass and they were lawn mowers. I knew then they were out to get me, so I tried out for the track team, a no-contact sport. I thought I was fast, but those kids were roadrunners. I'll never forget how Coach Benjamin kept working with me, telling me not to get discouraged. He was a real inspiration in my life. But that didn't last either, so what was next for me?

5

Uncle Sonny Richards

When I was fourteen, my parents had taken me to the Boulevard Nightclub in Queens to see my father's brother perform. His name was Sonny Richards, and I was really impressed by his broad talent—singing, dancing, and impressions. I was particularly impressed by his jokes because, before I ever saw my uncle perform, I used to send away for pictures of Sid Caesar, Milton Berle, Red Buttons, Steve Allen, etc. *Now I have an entertainer in the family,* I thought—and Uncle Sonny was as good as all of them.

I remember how impressed I was after seeing him at the Boulevard nightclub—so impressed that when my school was holding auditions for a play—an operetta called *The Red Mill*—I decided to give it a try. I auditioned for Mr. Prochilo, the drama teacher, and landed the lead.

And bingo—I'd finally found my niche. *This it what I should be doing—entertaining,* I thought. I did the show, and I enjoyed the reaction I received from the mixed audience—students, teachers, and parents. So now I was like Uncle Sonny—entertaining people and enjoying it. By the way, I should mention that this wasn't the first time I'd been on stage. I'd once played a teapot in a Salvation Army School production, when I was four.

I'd also appeared before an audience at JHS 162, when I was in a variety show put on by the senior class. I sang and did a comedy routine with my friend, Richie Mendolia. Apparently I'd always aspired to be a performer—it just didn't become clear to me until I did the play at PJHS. After that, the other classmates sort of warmed up to me a little more. They no longer saw me as a hood from Brooklyn, but just another classmate who wanted to be accepted.

Sadly, we lost Uncle Sonny in 1959. With his career climbing, he was headlining at the Fountain Bleau Hotel in Miami, Florida. He was in his dressing room getting ready for a show, when he suddenly had chest pains. A doctor was called in immediately, and they worked on him for ten minutes while they waited for the ambulance. By the time it got there, he'd died. There was nothing anyone could do—it was a massive heart attack. Uncle Sonny, the handsome, talented man I admired, was gone at forty-three years old.

6

A Gift for Mom and Dad, Boxing Gloves for Me

On September 19, 1955, Dad got a great birthday present when the little girl my mom always wanted was born. They named her Deborah Ann, and she and Dad would share the same birthday forever. Cute as a button she was, an adorable little girl, and now Stephen Junior would have a biological sister to grow up with. Boy was everyone ecstatic—another great day in our lives.

Meanwhile, it was high school, confraternity, hanging out at the Green Pavilion in Ronkonkoma, and wondering what was next for me. Then I saw an article in the *Daily News* about the Golden Gloves, so I thought, *Okay, I'll try that.* I signed up, and in 1956, I fought at Sunnyside Gardens in Queens. I had no representation, so I fought "unattached," as they called it. But they gave me corner men to help out. A corner man is the guy who gives you instructions on how to fight your opponent. They also take care of any cuts you might get during the fight.

No one I told I had a boxing match believed me—except for my parents and my Uncle Sonny, who had shown up at the fight and rooted me on. I lost the fight, but the next day I was taking a nap on the couch in the living room of our little mansion when Uncle Louis came in from next door hooting and hollering. "Hey, Sal—you made the papers." He was holding up the back page of the *Daily News,* and there I saw a half page with my picture on it, fighting the guy who beat me—Kenneth Fox. Then the phone started to ring, classmates who hadn't believed me were calling, as well as some of my other uncles, who said they would have been there for me but thought I was joking. Yeah, that'll teach them to listen to me, but that's okay because I DID IT, no matter what anybody said!

About three months later, I got a letter in the mail from the Olympic Boxing Team, asking me if I wanted to train with them for the Olympics. My reply was, "No thanks—been there, done that." And that was the end of my boxing career.

One day I met a guy who was putting a variety show together and wanted me to join them and go on the road—a chance to break into show business. I wound up quitting school in my senior year, just for the chance to be in this show. Well, don't you just know it, but I lost another "fight." The show did go into rehearsal, but then the producer skipped with the investors' money, and that ended that.

Then the shit hit the fan. "I told you so—don't quit school." "You'll never amount to anything. Why didn't you listen to me?" I couldn't blame them. They were only looking out for my well-being. So I thought, *I'll show them. No matter what they say, I'm going to make something of myself—they'll see.*

Now I was looking for a job, and I got a few—shoe salesman, construction worker, and record salesman. Those didn't last long because I lost interest very fast and had one thing on my mind—show business. At the end of 1957, I got a job at the Charcoal Ovens in Commack. I started as a short-order cook and worked my way up to manager. I wound up running the place. My dad used to come in for lunch a lot. By this time he had his own brake business nearby.

7

The Royal Aires—Doo-Wop Days

It was at the Charcoal Ovens that I hooked up with some guys who liked to hang out there, and one day, after the lunch rush, we started singing doo-wop, just for fun. But the more we sang, the more we liked what we heard; and the Royal Aires were born: Rudy, Ray, Frank, John, and me.

We started doing local shows, and then went to New York to seek a record deal. While we were doing background for a singer at a recording studio, one of the engineers told us he knew a guy who was looking for new groups. So we went to see Lee Clark, owner of Gallo Records. We auditioned for him, and he signed us to a record deal. We were as excited as kids in a candy store. We told our parents, and again I heard, "Better not quit your day job." We pursued the gig anyway. Our first recording was "Baby, Baby," backed with "Friendship Ring," then "You're in Love," backed with "Please Don't Leave Me Now."

So now we were recording artists, doing record hops all over the country to promote the group. We wound up with a two-sided hit in some of the New England states and a few in the South—"Baby, Baby" was number one, and "Friendship Ring" was number three on the charts in those areas. Then it started to get played in New York, on the Allen Freed Show—and if he played it, it would become a hit. But he didn't play it for long. Payola was big in those days, and the owner of Gallo Records refused to pay to have the record played, so it went off the charts quickly. When the second record was released, the same thing happened. We tried to keep going, doing shows around town, but when the kids didn't hear the record on the radio, they didn't show up. The group split up after two years, but we remained friends.

Since then, though, John has passed away, and Ray is in an incoherent way because of a bad auto accident. I haven't seen him or heard about him in many years. Frank moved upstate New York and became a hairstylist. Sadly, he recently passed away from pancreatic cancer. He was a good friend and I will miss him. Rudy went back to carpentry, his former profession. I see him occasionally, and he's a big, strong guy—and a great friend.

Meanwhile, I kept hearing the same old line from the family— "Get a Job!"

8

Getting a Job!

With nothing else to do, I got a job at Miles Shoe Store in Centereach, working every day while still trying to get some kind of gig
in the "biz." I was making $98 a week and commissions on polish and
other shoe products. It was the most frustrating time of my life, working a regular job, but that's what you had to do if you needed money.
Weekends I would hang out at the Windmill Club in Coram with my
best friend, Mike Greco. It was a rock-and-roll club, which Mike and
I eventually booked after we started a little R&R booking agency. We
would put local rock acts from the '50s in the club, and we were there
every weekend to make sure the gigs went well.

So I was in show business again, and all of a sudden we got calls
from other clubs in the area. We started to expand, and now we were
booking comics, singers, dancers, and other acts. We made ten percent of the salary we got for them. Some made fifty bucks, some
made more, but we were in business, and that's all that mattered. But I
thought to myself, *Hey—these people are making good money and
I'm splitting a few dollars with Mike.* So I started to look for a band to
work with in any capacity. After all, I could sing.

I started hanging out with the Johnny Jay Trio, a combo that
worked local clubs all over Long Island. I would go with them on jobs
and ask them to bring me up to sing a few songs, but act like I don't
know anything about it. It worked for a while, but the customers and
the bosses got wise and knew I was there to show off. It didn't hurt,
because I started to learn the ropes. I never got paid, but every once in
a while I got a turkey sandwich.

9

From a Raffle Ticket to a Wedding

One day my buddy Mike, who was a shop steward for A&P, called and asked me to go with him to a dinner-dance his union was having. I told him I was going to the Windmill. He said, "Take a ride with me—we'll go there later." He just had to show up and make an appearance at the dance. As it turned out, there was a band there, and when I saw that, I thought, *A chance to sing.* Sure enough, I knew the bandleader and asked him to bring me up as a guest. I sang, and I got my rocks off.

As Mike and I were having dinner, this beautiful girl walked over to the table. I figured she was coming to tell me how great I was, but boy was I wrong. She was selling raffle tickets and asked if we wanted to buy any. I asked, "How much?"

She said, "Fifty cents apiece."

I said, "If you're the prize, I'll buy the whole book." She looked at me like I was crazy and stormed off in a huff.

After a while, just as Mike and I were ready to leave, we heard someone singing "Some of These Days," an old song made famous by Sophie Tucker, the Last of the Red Hot Mamas. We looked up, and there was the raffle girl, dressed in a tight gold lamé dress, even more stunning than when I first saw her. When she finished singing, I approached her, gave her my card, and told her we were running a show and dance at a club in Ronkonkoma. "Would you like to sing in our show?" I asked.

She said, "I don't know," and walked away. She probably hated me.

I found out her name was RoseAnn and asked a girlfriend of hers to get her number for me. When I got it, I called for weeks, but she never took the call. Her mother kept telling her that it was someone named Sal, but she refused to come to the phone. I met one of her girlfriends, who happened to be in the same union, and I begged her to call and tell her I was trying to reach her. She did, and RoseAnn said, "That was him calling? I thought it was this other Sal I knew, and I didn't want to talk to him." I called her again and we made a date.

Ready for history? We were married eight months later, and we're still married today.

We had it tough in the beginning, and it started at our wedding. We didn't get enough, as they say, "boosters" to pay for the wedding. Boosters are the gift envelopes you receive, hopefully with enough money in them. We went into the bridal suite and counted the "take." Not enough to pay for the wedding. So Uncle Louie, her father, my father, and a few others passed the hat, until we finally had enough to get out of the building with a little left over for the honeymoon. The party was great. RoseAnn and I got up and sang some Louie Prima songs, and the family loved it. She grabbed her tiara from her head and threw it out to the crowd. I said to myself, *I have married my match.* When we finished, we didn't know that passersby had stopped to watch us. When we got off, some of the people asked how much we got for a performance. I said that we were the bride and groom and hadn't been hired to perform. It was funny.

We spent our honeymoon at Williams Lake Hotel, in upstate New York. It was May 1, and the season hadn't started yet. The place was empty, except for three other couples. We did our best to have fun, but it wasn't a place for a honeymoon. We decided to leave, but instead of going home, we drove to Washington, DC. That was better. We got to see all the sights and monuments, and we had a great time.

10

Lost My Job

Honeymoon over, we headed back home. I had the job in a shoe store in Oakdale, and I couldn't wait to get back to making money. When we got home and I collected the mail, I found a letter from the store: "You have been replaced—come and pick up your last check." *WHAT?*

We'd been living in Patchogue and were just making the rent. I went on unemployment, getting $30 a week and trying to find work— and RoseAnn got pregnant. One night, when she was in her eighth month, she went into labor. I rushed her to Brookhaven Hospital, where she delivered a boy. Premature, the baby was only three pounds and was in an incubator. Ro was in the hospital for about four days, and when it was time for her to go home, the doctors said we had to leave the baby for care. He'd passed the crisis and there was no need for us to stay. They said they would take care of him. So, we went home.

The next morning, Ro asked me to call to see how the baby was doing. I had to go to the corner store and call because we didn't have a phone. When I called, I got the shock of my life. The hospital told me that the baby had expired at 9:00 A.M. I said, "Why wasn't I informed?" They said, "You have no phone. We're so sorry, but his lungs collapsed."

Now I had to go tell RoseAnn. But what would I say? How would I do it? When I walked in the apartment, she asked how things were.

But she could tell by my face that something was wrong. I said, "They had a problem," and she screamed, "He's dead, isn't he?" There was nothing more to say after that.

By that time, her parents and mine had arrived at the apartment— I'd called them before I returned. Everyone was devastated, to say the least. Our parents were consoling us, but at the same time they were hurting too. We were still just kids. What a way to start a life together.

11

How Did This Happen?

So here we were, a couple of married kids living in an upstairs apartment in Patchogue, Long Island. No job, no money, devastated from the loss our first born…what the fuck? This wasn't how it was supposed to be. If it weren't for our parents, I don't know what we would have done. Time moved slowly, and the $30 weekly unemployment checks were not nearly enough to survive. Sure I'd had some jobs—construction, shoe sales, vacuum cleaner salesman—you name it, I'd tried it. But as hard as I tried, I just could not hold a job for long. So we couldn't pay the rent, and we were evicted.

We went to live with my brother-in-law, Tom, and his wife, Claudia, for a while. In the meantime, the show biz bug was biting me more and more. I put a band together, and even put Tom in the group. We called ourselves the Looney Tunes. We did club dates, weddings, and nightclubs, getting $20 a man per night. Now what the hell could I buy with that—especially working only one or two nights a week? But I continued, and we were finally able to move from Tommy's place. Thank God for them helping us in the meantime.

It was now 1963, and we found a cheap house in Ronkonkoma—three rooms and one bath for Ro and me—and, since Ro was pregnant again, our soon-to-be-born son, Sal Junior. I was now doing comedy—emcee work in local clubs around the Island and in Brooklyn. But it still wasn't enough to support a family, so at the same time I worked at a service station, pumping gas and doing oil changes five days a week. On weekends I played the local clubs.

12

A Christmas Gift

Salvatore Giovia, Jr., was born on December 26, 1963, the day after Christmas. What a gift from God he was, a beautiful child who looked just like his beautiful mom. Now I really had my work cut out for me, so it was time to get a regular job.

Once again, Tommy helped me, getting me a job selling Kirby vacuum cleaners. I found that to be a most disgusting way to make a living, talking people into believing that this was the miracle machine for them, selling it to people without rugs—or money, for that matter. It was an expensive piece of shit—but hey, somebody had to do it. I'd get them to sign the contract—and bingo, I made a $100 commission.

Now we we're on the move again. Unable to pay the $80-a-month rent, we were evicted from our apartment. We eventually found a house on Ann Road, in Centereach. Wow! It was great—two bedrooms, two baths, living room, kitchen, and a playroom. How did I swing that? Well, I guess my ability as a salesman paid off because I convinced the owners that I was making good money. They were very nice, and rented it to us for $150 a month; they didn't know that I had to borrow the money to pay for the first month's rent. But as time went by, I could afford the rent because I was selling vacuum cleaners *and* working at nightclubs on weekends.

That was in 1965, and we were on our way up. We painted the house inside and out, made it our mansion, and treated it like it was ours—mowing the lawn, keeping it spotless, etc. By the way, guess who lived down the street? Tommy and Claudia. They'd moved there from Hempstead—and, yes, they'd told us that the house was for rent. I guess we were continuing the trend our parents started.

Oh—I almost forgot to mention that RoseAnn was pregnant again. On April 1, 1965, Guy John Giovia was born. He was a rugged little son of a gun, and he looked just like me! By this time I'd put a trio, the Club Daters, together. The other two members were Johnny Box on accordion and Phil Nardone on drums—two musicians I'd met in some of the places I'd worked. I played the bass, which I faked—and I was so bad that my accordion player said, "Don't ever turn that amp on." I never did.

Since I didn't have a car, I had to hitchhike to and from the gig every night. We were performing at The Marc Terrace in Hicksville, and one night I started hitching toward home at 3:00 A.M. I got a ride on a *Daily News* delivery truck, and the driver said he would take me all the way to Centereach, but since he'd just started his route, I'd have to go on the run with him. I said sure—anything to get home.

By the third stop, I was helping the guy toss bundles of papers off the back of the truck to the waiting delivery guys. Did I mention I was wearing a tux? Well, one of the guys on the receiving end of the papers looked at me funny, maybe wondering if this was a new thing, a guy in a tuxedo tossing them their bundles, thinking maybe the price was going to go up. As it turned out, I met this driver every night for a month and always got to Centereach safely. What an experience.

13

The Catskills

By 1967 I was doing club dates as a comic emcee around Long Island and Brooklyn. One day I got a call from Johnny Martinelli, an agent who booked some of the resort hotels in the Italian Alps, as we called that part of the Catskill Mountains. He booked me to open for Lou Monte, an Italian singing star who had a few hit records, mostly novelty songs. One of his biggest hits was called "Pepino the Mouse," which he'd introduced on the Ed Sullivan Show.

So there I was, on my way to the Villa Maria, a popular resort in Haines Falls, New York. Was I excited to be opening for Lou Monte? You bet I was. I left my house at 5:00 A.M. that morning so I wouldn't be late. I had a car now, a '53 Buick, and I was worried that it might overheat or break down. This was an opportunity I didn't want to miss. Well, the car was fine and I arrived at the hotel at 8:00 A.M.—a little early, since the guests were just getting up for breakfast. When I went to check in, the owner was at the desk. She asked me what I was doing there so early, since the show didn't start until 9:00 P.M. I said, "I worked in the area last night and got up early." Of course that was a lie. Anyway, I checked in, had breakfast, and hung around all day. About three in the afternoon, Lou Monte arrived for rehearsal. I went to the club and there he was with his guitar, ready to rehearse. We got acquainted, and we remained friends until his passing many years later.

That night, the show went on at nine. I did thirty minutes and went over well with the crowd, which was a relief. Needless to say, though, Lou killed them. After the show, we hung out till early morning, just talking and mingling with the guests. It was a two-day booking, so the next day, I hung around the pool and entertained a lot of the guests, doing some schtick and making them laugh.

That night the club was open to outsiders as well as hotel guests, and the place filled up. The owners, Frank and Lyda DiNino, were very happy about that, to say the least. I became friendly with them, and after talking awhile they asked me to stay one more night for an extra $50 bucks. They wanted me to do a game night on Sunday with the guests because their social director had quit two days before I got there. So I did it, and the next day, they offered me a job as a social director for ten weeks in the summer. I figured what the hell—a steady gig. Why not?

When I got home, I told RoseAnn about it the offer.

She said, "What about me and the kids?"

I said, "No problem—you can come with me." So we packed up and I went back to the Villa Maria, this time with my family. I was now a social director, playing games with the guests and arranging activities for them. On weekends I got to perform at night. When they booked a comic, I opened as a singer, and when they booked a singer, I opened as a comic. What great training it was for me. Eventually I got gigs at other hotels in the same area for some extra cash. I was only making $300 a week, working from 8:00 A.M. till midnight. During the day it was games, while after dinner in the club it was talent night, masquerade night, things like that. I ran it all. On the weekends, it was show time.

This went on for four years. Every year, as I drove up to the mountains, I'd pass signs on the highway advertising hotels in the Borscht Belt, the Jewish side of the Catskills. I'd see the names of the stars that would be appearing there—Red Buttons, Milton Berle, Steve and Edie. I thought, *Someday my name will be on one of those signs.*

One day in 1968 I was getting a haircut, preparing to leave for a gig. The barber Jimmy Tullo started to tell me about a new cable TV company starting up in Selden. He said, "There is a guy looking to do some local programming out of the new studio. He is Arthur Gusow and he is the manager of the company."

I called and made an appointment to meet Mr. Gusow. The company was owned by Manhattan Cable, and they were soliciting to install cablevision to homeowners in the area.

They did not have any local programming; the only thing they offered at the time was better TV reception and this new movie channel called HBO.

I told Mr. Gusow of my idea to do a localized variety show from the studio, which was a storefront next to a pizza parlor in a strip mall. He liked the idea and we made a deal. I put a show together and started the first live variety show on cable.

We had a live band with friends of mine, Mike Alessi, sax; Joe Chirco, drums; Charlie Martone, guitar; and Frank Palladino, bass. They would play an opening theme song and played for some of the singing guests we had on the show, and for me should I decide to sing.

I interviewed different guests every week on Thursday night from 6:30 to 8:00 P.M. We had to finish by 8:00, because the band and I belonged to a bowling league and we had to be there by 9:00 P.M.

Some of the guest we had were comedians Pat Cooper, Godfrey Cambridge, and some local comics. The singing guests were Liza Minnelli, and The De John Sisters, to name a few.

People who did not have the service would come to the strip mall and watch the show through the front window, eventually the company started to get subscribers so they could watch our show.

We also had some local politicians, restaurant owners, dog trainers. You name it, we had it.

The show got so popular that we moved it to a nightclub in Ronkonkoma, The Suffolk House. Tony Braile was the owner and a dear friend of mine, and he welcomed the idea of doing some shows from his club.

The show lasted for two years, cable was starting to grow, Arthur Gusow tried to farm out our shows to other cable companies, but they had their own ideas, so we were history, and as you know now cable is the giant in broadcasting.

I wish I had the videos of those shows.

Oh! If I knew then!

14

Finally—A Break

At the end of 1971, I was doing club dates around the New York area and got a booking at Carl Hoppel's Valley Stream Park Inn. There was a girl singer in the show named Bunny Parker. Her husband, Tony Marino, was her musical director. She opened the show and stayed around to watch me perform, and after the show we all sat and had coffee together. That started a friendship that's lasted to this day.

About a week later, I got a call from the Rapp Agency in New York. They were the top bookers in the Catskills. Although I'd never worked for them before, they asked me to do a gig for them at the Laurels Hotel. Apparently someone who frequented the Laurels had seen my show at Carl Hoppel's. He told the entertainment director, Sid Fish, about me, and suggested he book me. As if that wasn't enough, my new friends, Bunny and Tony, were already working the Catskills, and they'd also told Sid about me.

Sid called the Rapp office and asked about a new guy named Sal Richards, saying he wanted to give him a try. So they booked me in a late show, which went on at 1:00 A.M., and they put Bunny Parker on to open for me. When I showed up I was nervous as hell, but when I saw Bunny and Tony, my anxiety eased a little. I went on after Bunny finished her show, and sitting ringside was Charlie Rapp, the owner of the agency. Howie Rapp, his nephew, and a few other agents from his office, were with them.

Holy shit! Just what I needed—my first time in the Catskills, where stars were born, and these guys were sitting right in front. It was make-it-or-break-it time now. So I pulled myself together, went on—and, with the help of God, I killed 'em and got a standing ovation. After the show, Howie Rapp came over to me and said, "Come with us—we're going to the coffee shop." When I walked into the coffee shop, the guests started applauding and giving me accolades. I was stunned, ever grateful that it all went well.

So there I was, sitting at a table with the big-shots from the Rapp office, who were telling me not to talk to anyone else about bookings and so forth. Then Sid Fish came over and said he decided he wanted me back the following week in the main show. I was thrilled, and after a few days, the Rapp agency signed me to a contract for twenty shows for the summer season. They did this through an agent I had in Long Island, who shall remain nameless because he turned out to be a snake in the business and does not deserve to be mentioned. What a crook he was. He'd charge the client three times what he gave me, and then charge me a commission on top of that.

Anyway, the rest is history. I didn't do just twenty shows that season—I did a total of eighty. Sounds like a lot, but when you're young and hungry, it was easy. Besides, the money did not start off all that great. But it was a start, working two shows a night, a hotel at ten, a bungalow colony at 12:30, and some Saturdays doing three shows in one night.

I remember working a hotel called the Echo in the early years. The musical director, whose name was Steve Michaels, was only fourteen! I looked at him and wondered, *What does this kid know about conducting?* Well, let me tell you something—he did an excellent job, and later he became my steady conductor. Not only was he a great musician, but he also became a good friend. RoseAnn and I are honored to say we baptized his daughter, Michelle, some years later. His wife, Lorraine, and son, Brandon, went on to become family. And when I needed musical advice, or some understanding when things went bad, Steve was always right on target.

15

It's Starting to Come Together

In 1972, the Rapp Agency had an awards dinner at the Friars Club in New York to honor outstanding performers for the season. I won the Charlie Award for Outstanding Comic in 1972, following in the footsteps of such former winners as Totie Fields, Norm Crosby, and many others. What an accomplishment for a kid from Brooklyn, who had a dream that was gradually coming true. The next thing I knew, I was a headliner at all the major resorts in the Catskills—the Concord, Kutschers, Brickman, Raleigh, Nevele, Fallsview, and so on. Oh, by the way—my name would be on some of the billboards a few years later. I told you!

Now I was on my way, doing shows everywhere, and in 1973 I got a call to open for Harold Melvin and The Blue Notes at the world-famous Copacabana, in New York City. It was a nine-day engagement, with two shows a night, and all my friends showed up to support me. Joe Cohen, a reviewer from *Variety,* caught the show and gave me my first review ever—and it was a great one. I was higher than a kite over that.

When I found out that I was going to open at the Copa, I wanted to go in big. I spoke to Dave Gross, a pianist and conductor I'd met while working the Villa Roma in Calicoon, New York, and asked him to come and conduct for me. He was an accomplished musician for his age—eighteen!—with a lot of talent. He accepted, and we were together for many years. Dave got an offer to conduct and travel with a famous singing duo, Sandler and Young. I was not going to stand in his way because he wasn't making the money with me that he could make with them. He toured with them for a few years, then started playing for Bobby Vinton, which he still does. He still plays for me at times when Steve Michaels can't do a gig.

In 1977 I did the Merv Griffin Show from Caesars Palace in Las Vegas. That wasn't an easy gig to get. I'd auditioned once before in a room with two people, and they said okay, do your act. I started and got no reaction at all, so I stopped after a minute and said I couldn't audition this way, that I needed an audience. So they said, make the arrangements and we'll come to see you. I went to Jilly's, a famous celebrity hangout in New York, Frank Sinatra's favorite place. I knew the manager, so I asked him if I could use the room to audition. He said yes, and I stacked the room four days later. The talent coordinators came, I did my show, and I got the Merv Griffin gig. I also had appearances on a few TV shows—*Make Me Laugh, The Comedy Shop* with Norm Crosby, and *Dean Martin's Comedy World.* Wow. I was cooking that year and starting to get some recognition. Then, because of the exposure I'd been getting, I was chosen to do one of the first comedy shows on HBO. It was called the "Catskill Comedians," and it was hosted by Joey Bishop. And there were no four-letter words allowed. I was on with Jackie Wakefield, Corbett Monica, Jack Eagle, Gus Christi, and Al Bernie. We each did a twenty-minute spot and the show was a hit when it aired.

The only problem was, not too many people subscribed to HBO in those days, and the audience was thin. But I did the show, and it was another notch in my arsenal of comedy. That didn't mean I was a star—I continued to work in the Catskills for many years after that— but it certainly was a stepping-stone. I went on to work places like the Top Hat in Franklin Square, the San Su San in Mineola, Carl Hoppel's, the Moulin Rouge in Staten Island, and nightclubs throughout the country. All those places are gone now, but what an era it was.

Oh, and let's not forget working the Florida condominiums. These were retirement complexes, with all the amenities, including 1,500-seat theatres and country clubs. In-season they would have a different show every night. In the beginning, the pay wasn't terrific, but after a few years, I made good money. I worked there every two years. I'd get a contract to do twenty shows at all the venues, and it was a great experience. The booker paid for airfare, hotel accommodations, and local transportation. Yes, sir—that was show business—all made possible through the Charles Rapp agency.

When I worked the condo circuit in Florida, I used Mark Friedman, a guy I met on a gig. He played the show for me and a singer named Rodi Alexander. I liked him so much that I wound up using him on all my condo gigs, and some of the cruises I did on Royal Caribbean. He's since married Rodi, and they have a wonderful son, Daryn. We're all very close. I often requested Rodi to open for me, first because she is a terrific talent, and second, it kept her and Mark close.

Working the cruise ships was a new thing for me, staying on a ship for a week at a time and doing two shows a night. The theater had a great stage, great lighting, great sound, and a great band—just like Vegas. But when the show was over, I was stuck on the ship for however long it took for the ship to get back to the port. Sometimes they flew me back from other countries or flew me in, and I would stay overnight until the ship arrived the next day.

I did this for ten years on Royal Caribbean, doing ten ships a year with no problem. When you worked a ship, you had to be careful not to offend anyone, or you were out. I remember a few years ago, in 2007, I was working one of their ships and met the cruise director. His name escapes me…deliberately. His vibe announced that he was the big shot and he was doing me a favor. Believe me, they're not all like that, just this chubby palooka. Mark felt the same way when he was with me. It was all about Mr. Chubby, and he'd rush the rehearsal so he could rehearse his opening song. Hah. The palooka couldn't even sing.

The cruise line had comment cards that the passengers filled out at the end of the cruise. I did two shows and killed 'em, got standing ovations. After each show, I went into the lobby with Mark, and signed and sold fifty DVDs of one of my previously taped shows (I'll get to those later), with the ship getting thirty percent of the sales. I said to Mark, "So let them take their percentage—it gets me out there."

After that, Mark and I went up to Johnny Rockets for a hamburger. There we bumped into guests, who came over to us and complimented both of us on a great show.

The next morning we flew home, and I said to Mark, "See you next week." See, we had seven more contract ships to do that season.

When I got home, there was a message from the Casino Agency to call them. I did, and they told me that Royal Caribbean had cancelled the rest of my tour. "What? Why?" They told me that the cruise director had written them a letter saying that I wasn't good for their ship, that there were too many complaints. Bullshit. They taped all the shows, so why not get those tapes and prove we did badly? Were they kidding? After ten years? The a-hole cruise director did not like the quality of our shows and probably was pissed that Mark and I did great. I always had Mark do a featured spot in my show, singing, playing piano, and thoroughly entertaining the crowd. It always worked before, so I didn't want to hear that the guests did not like the show.

It was, in my opinion, restraint of trade, and I thought I might make a case out of it. But then I decided, *It's their loss.* "They'll come back," I said.

16

Me and the Mob

There was a time early in my career when I was approached by some "connected" guys who wanted to manage me. It was around 1975, about the time I was working the San Su San in Mineola. Knowing who they were, I was a little afraid to say no. They offered me stardom. Their incentives to handle me? A recording contract, movies, television, and many other rewards.

I considered doing it for a while, and I discussed it with RoseAnn. I said, "Is this the right move? I've heard so many stories about things like this and I am concerned." I had known entertainers who'd done this and wound up with no career. They owned you. You had to do a lot of favors for some of their friends—weddings, birthdays, and parties—for free. And you were always at their beck and call. Think Johnny Fontane, the singer in *The Godfather,* who had to perform at the wedding of Don Corleone's daughter as a favor for a favor.

As time went by, I did what I could to avoid conversations with them about such an arrangement and made up excuses: "I really don't want to be a star—this is just a side thing for me," or, "I am already married and I don't think I could be married to this thing."

Eventually they got the hint and gradually backed off, but one thing was sure—they were legit fans and always came to see me perform. One night in 1975, I was appearing at the San Su San in Mineola Long Island, a favorite hangout for these guys. I was opening for Julius LaRosa, a singer who was discovered by Arthur Godfrey while

35

he was in the navy. He was a star, and I was thrilled to be on the bill with him. We became friends and have been ever since. But anyway, there were my mob fans, all sitting ringside. After my show, I hung out at the bar and spoke with these guys but only as an entertainer talking to fans. I was never associated with them on a business level.

I had a more frightening encounter with the mob toward the end of the 1980s. I was headlining at La Maganette restaurant and nightclub on 50th Street and Third Avenue in Manhattan, a great place to go for great food, a floor show, and to see and be seen. The owners were good friends of mine and booked me there a lot.

One particular night, after I finished my show, I was approached by a made guy I'd heard about. He had just been released from prison the week before. He said to me, "I was sent by the old man, and he wants you to take out the impression you do of Frank Sinatra Junior." I said that I'd been doing it for a long time and it never bothered anyone before.

He said, "Well it bothers me, and I want you to take it out or else."

I tried to tell him it was done in fun and not meant to defame anyone. He stopped me cold and said, "Shut up. I don't give a fuck why you do it. Are you listening to me?"

It was starting to get loud, and my Sicilian brain wasn't thinking clearly. I wasn't about to take any shit from anyone, but what a jerk I was to have an attitude like that with this guy. A lot of my fans were there to see me, and when they heard the commotion they piled out like there was going to be a murder. The bosses came over and settled it down for a while.

RoseAnn was with me, and we went upstairs to the bar to settle down and have a drink. The guy was at the other end of the bar with some other Goodfellas, and they called me over to talk about it. For a while we all got along great, but the more this guy drank, the worse he got, and he started all over again. The owner of the club said, "Sal, maybe you should leave." He paid me and off I went.

As we were getting our coats from the hat check, one of the Goodfellas said to me, "He wants you to call him tomorrow and meet him at the bakery for a sit-down." *Holy shit—I am a dead man,* I thought. RoseAnn was so frightened that she started to cry. On the way home I made a call to one of my old friends from the San Su San. I told him what happened and who the guy was. He said, "I'll take care of it." I didn't really think he would do that for me though.

Anyway, I called the guy who'd threatened me the next day to arrange the sit-down he'd wanted. He told me, "Forget about it. I was drunk and I was wrong for the way I handled the situation. You don't have to come." What a relief that was!

I couldn't believe it. It was like a scene from a movie, almost like it was a script. My friend had come through and hadn't asked for any favor in return. As they say, "You never know who your friends are."

All these guys are gone now. Some are dead, some are retired with new names, and some are just missing, maybe having a drink with Jimmy Hoffa somewhere.

Meanwhile, as you read the next few chapters, you'll be amazed by the things that caused me to wonder, *Why us?*

17

What the Hell Did I Do?

Well, I was on my way, working clubs, resorts, Florida, cruises, and many other venues. I thought this was the life, doing things I should never have done—staying out late, drinking, gambling, etc. You figure out the "et cetera." I don't want to remind my wife about what went on when she reads this book. Anyway, it finally caught up to me. RoseAnn decided that I'd gone over the edge and she couldn't live this way anymore. We fought constantly over my disregard for my family, and she up and left me—took the kids and moved into an apartment in Hauppauge. The lawyers worked out the separation papers, and that was that. I paid child support and did the best I could to help them so they could live comfortably.

After a while, I couldn't take it anymore. I loved her and my boys too much, and I wanted to try to get back together. It was a struggle, because RoseAnn was afraid to take a chance on me. I actually begged her, and I even slept on the floor outside her apartment night after night, hoping she'd listen to me. Sal Junior and Guy didn't understand why we weren't together. To them it was, "Daddy's on the road, working."

One night she opened the door and said, "Come on in. You can't sleep on the floor anymore. It doesn't look right, and the neighbors are talking." I slept on the couch that night. When the boys woke in the morning and saw me, they yelled, "Daddy's home!" They were so excited to see me—and for me, seeing them was a dream come true.

But it wasn't all peaches and cream yet. Ro and I still had a few things to work out, so we went to Father Rocco, a priest we knew from the Assumption Church in Centereach. We spoke for a while, and I confessed that I was the one who'd caused the breakup, that RoseAnn was just looking for me to stop what I was doing and live a normal life. Father Rocco made a few suggestions and we listened to him carefully. My beautiful and loving RoseAnn was distraught, and I could see the doubt in her mind.

After we got in the car, we drove around in silence for a while. Finally I asked the question, fearing the worst. "So what do you think, Honey? Will you give me another shot at this? I love you with all my heart, and I know you love me. I'm sorry for all the hurt I caused, and I'll do my best to make it up to you." When she was silent for a while, I tried to lighten it up a little and said, "If you take me back, I'll run down Jericho Turnpike with bells on."

She gave me one of her beautiful smiles, then after making me sweat a little longer, she said, "Okay!" Then after she set the rules, I pulled into a strip mall. I went into a hardware store and bought cow bells and any bells I could get my hands on, threw them around my neck, went to the car window and said, "You drive—follow me."

"You're crazy," She said, but she followed me as I asked her to, and there I went, running down Jericho Turnpike with bells on. Naturally, a lot of other drivers were blowing their horns at me, but what do you expect? New York drivers aren't exactly known for their patience.

After a while I got in the car and we went to my mother's house, where the boys were, to tell her the news—and the tears fell like rain. Sal Junior and Guy wanted to know why we were crying. RoseAnn said, "These are happy tears. Daddy is coming back to live with us!"

18

Life Goes On

I got a weekday job at Harwyn Shoes, and on weekends I continued to do clubs. It was now 1971. Then, I got a call from Lou DiGiaimo Casting and was informed that they were casting a movie called *The Godfather.* It seemed like they were auditioning every Italian in New York, and I was one of them. I was lucky to get a small role—a drunk at the wedding—with sixteen shooting days in Staten Island. It was so exciting to meet Marlon Brando and the rest of the cast, and the only thing that seemed to matter was that I was in the company of greatness.

On the set I was upgraded to a larger role, which was later cut, but I *can* be seen for a brief moment in that wedding scene. I still get residual checks every time the movie is shown. And that was the start of my movie career. Incidentally, my next role came in 1975—in the film *The Valachi Papers,* with Charles Bronson—and the one after that was in 1981. What a gap between roles. Good thing I had comedy to fall back on—or selling shoes, doing roofing or concrete work, selling vacuums, anything to supplement my income while waiting to become a "star."

So now we were one happy family again. We stayed at the apartment for a year. It was 1973 now, and I was driving around in a 1961 Pontiac—all I could afford. But as time went by, I started working more and earning more, so it was time for a new car. I applied for a lease on a 1973 Lincoln Town Car—and holy shit, I was approved. I flew to Philadelphia to pick up the car, and as I drove it back to Long Island, I felt like a king.

When I got home, RoseAnn, Sal, and Guy came running outside, all grinning from ear to ear. We were finally moving up in the world, but now I had to make more money so I could afford the big white Lincoln. Then, of course, because our apartment wasn't suitable for a family on the way up, Ro wanted to move to a house. She found a nice one in Lake Grove—three bedrooms, two baths, living room, dining room, kitchen, and a large den with a fireplace. And are you ready for this?—a twenty-by-forty-foot in-ground pool, fenced in. Now how the hell would we afford that?

Surprisingly, the rent on this house was $470 a month, with an option to buy. Could it be possible—all that for so little? It was, after all, 1978 by now. After a year, the owners were ready to sell and asked us if they could show the house through a realtor. True to their word, though, they did give us the option to buy it. When we asked how much, they quoted us a price of $50,000. We offered what we thought we could afford—$44,000. Well, we got lucky. The owners were now living in Arizona, and because they were living so far away, they wanted to avoid any hassle. So…it was *ours!*

19

"I Am Woman, Hear Me Roar"—*WHAT?*

Now it was late September 1980. Pete Cavallo, the promoter at the 86th Street Theater in Brooklyn, called me and asked, "Sal, are you available next Saturday? I have Helen Reddy coming in and ticket sales are slow. I thought maybe you could draw some people."

I told Pete I had a gig in the Catskills, but I would see if I could move it.

Thanks to the Rapp Agency. I was able to move the date. I let Pete know, and he informed me that I would be doing the first half of the show, and that I should do forty minutes. He had gotten approval from the William Morris Agency, who represented Helen Reddy. It was okay to use the band to do my impressions and a closing song.

On the day of the show, I was in the theater rehearsing the band with my conductor, Sal Sicari when one of Helen's people came by and asked me what I was doing. I explained that I was rehearsing for my portion of the show for that night. The next thing I knew, Jeff Wald, Helen's husband and manager, approached and said, "No way this is happening." I was confused because this had been approved already.

"What's the problem?" I asked. He told me that there would be no band on stage before Helen came on, and that was that.

I went to Pete, the promoter, and told him what was going on. He spoke with Jeff Wald, who continued to insist that it wasn't going to happen. Pete said to him, "Oh this is happening, all right—you don't run my theater." After a little discussion, Mr. Wald agreed that I could use the band, but the curtain had to be closed.

I said, "Are you kidding me? How can I do a show and get cues to my conductor with the curtain closed?" Pete decided to take Mr. Wald to the lobby and have a talk with him. That must have done the trick because Wald suddenly agreed to Pete's terms.

The show started at 8:00 P.M. My dear friend, Bobby Colt, opened the show with a song and then acted as emcee for the evening. After he introduced me, I did my forty-minute show, and the crowd was terrific. On this night I had decided to close with a song. While I was singing, I went into the audience and started to shake hands with the people in the first row. Suddenly I came across then-Governor Hugh Carey. I was surprised to see him, and I said, "Wow—Governor Carey. Nice to see you, Sir." I shook his hand, got back on stage, and finished my song—"You're Nobody Till Somebody Loves You."

As I walked backstage, Helen Reddy was standing there. She looked at me and said, "You'll never work in the business again." I didn't understand what she meant, so I ignored her remark and went up to my dressing room with my wife and a few friends. We had some coffee and snacks while waiting for the show to end. When Helen finished, you could tell from the sound of the ovation that she'd had a great performance.

Ro, my friends, and I started to walk down the stairs to meet some other friends, and as we went down Helen was coming up. She gave me a body block, like a defensive end, and said again, "You're out of the business. I'm telling Frank about you, and you're done."

"Frank who?" I asked.

"Sinatra—that's who," she said.

Hah. Like Mr. Sinatra would care about this.

RoseAnn walked over to her and asked, "Why are you treating my husband this way?" In response, Helen tossed the drink she had in her hand at my wife and called her a filthy name. Then she grabbed Ro by the hair, pulled her close, and the hit her in the breast. When RoseAnn started to defend herself, I headed toward the action—and Helen's bodyguard grabbed my wife by the throat. I jumped on him and beat him to a pulp. Meanwhile, Jeff Wald came running down the stairs with a knife in his hand. I looked up and yelled to one on my friends,

"He has a knife!" My friend kicked him in the balls so hard that he dropped the knife, and I don't think he pissed for a week.

By this time the police had been called, and when they arrived Pete explained what had happened—he'd seen the whole thing. I insisted that they arrest Helen, Jeff, and the bodyguard for assault and battery. The police took them all to the station house—including, unfortunately their ten-year-old son—and told us to come to sign a complaint.

At the precinct we're in one room and they're in another. As the sergeant was writing up the complaint, a cop came into our room and told me I had a phone call. When I grabbed the phone, lo and behold it was Governor Carey. He told me what a great show I'd done and the blah, blah, blah bullshit, until he got to the reason for his call. He said to me, "Sal, why don't you forget about this? They're friends of mine—they have their boy with them. Can't you let this go away?"

I said, "Sorry, but they attacked my wife—and no one attacks my wife and gets away with it. So, no, Mr. Carey—I won't let this go away. Thanks for calling."

Well, the calls kept coming, with the same requests to let them go. Finally he calls RoseAnn, and plays the little-boy's-with-them card. My wife, being a softy when it came to kids, asked me to try and work it out. So I got on the phone, and the governor suggested that we all get together for breakfast the following morning and settle this thing. He told me he was staying at the Essex House in New York and to call his liaison in the morning to arrange a time to meet.

So everyone went home, I dropped the charges, and Sunday morning I made the call. I was told, "Mr. and Mrs. Carey are at church, please call back in an hour." That seemed reasonable, so I called back—and this time, "He is out jogging—call in an hour." *Uh-oh— something is fishy here,* I thought. Well, I called back, and this time I was told, "The Governor had to get back to Albany on business. He suggested you take this up civilly." I tried to reach Helen Reddy, who ironically was staying at the same hotel, and was told, "They checked out early to catch a flight to LA."

I said to RoseAnn, "We've been had. There was never going to be a meeting, and they used their connections for a get-out-of jail-free card. Son of a bitch—what a moron I was to believe this shit. In the business, Wald and Reddy had a terrible reputation for fighting with people. I knew that, and I let this happen. RoseAnn had a big piece of her hair ripped out, and for years she suffered pains on her breast. So she decided to sue, and years later settled.

The *New York Post* had a full page article the next day, with a quote from Pete Cavallo: "This woman, who played a nun in the movies, had the mouth of a truck driver, and what they did to Sal and Rose-Ann was horrible. She will never be welcomed back to our theater again, but Sal Richards is always welcome."

I saw her twenty years later at a birthday party for Red Buttons—she was sitting at a table across from mine. I was with Connie Stevens and Lainie Kazan, who'd been friends for years. I'd noticed her looking my way, on a number of occasions, with an I-know-that-guy look on her face. There was a moment when she was by herself, so I walked over and said, "Do you know me?"

"Are you one of my old boyfriends?" she asked.

"Definitely not," I said. "My name is Sal Richards." She looked like she'd seen a ghost, then got up and walked to the other side of the room. Good riddance.

20

What the Hell Happened?

I was working the Catskills more and more. The money was getting better because I was doing some commercials, too. RoseAnn, being the most wonderful mother and wife, made sure everyone was doing well. She arranged pool parties, and Christmas and New Year's were always at our house, with the family and friends enjoying life. This was what it was supposed to be all about—a home filled with so much love. Her parents came up from Florida every summer to stay with us, too. What wonderful people they were, so giving and understanding and loving.

At the end of November 1980, it all came to an end. One morning I went upstairs to wake Sal Junior for school. At first I couldn't budge him, but when he finally opened his eyes and turned over, I saw blood dripping from his mouth. Thinking it was dental related, we took him to a dentist. But there was nothing wrong with his teeth, and the dentist suggested we see our family doctor. The doctor did some blood tests and said he'd call when he had the results. By the time we got home, Sal looked very tired, and there were dark pouches under his eyes.

The phone rang at 10:00 P.M. that evening, and it was the doctor. Little did we know that Sal picked up the phone at the same time and also heard these devastating words: "I'm sorry to tell you this—the tests came back and it appears that Sal Junior has leukemia." We heard a scream from upstairs, and we ran right up. Sal said, "I'm

going to die." Ro and I tried to calm him down with the usual assur-
ances—maybe they're wrong, maybe you'll just need more tests.

The next morning, we were at Mather Hospital. Sal had a bone
marrow test, which confirmed the leukemia. We called our dear
friend, Father Frank Pizzerelli, of Hope House Ministries, to come
talk to Sal and try to ease some of the worry.

The next day, we were at Sloan Kettering Cancer Hospital in Manhattan, which the oncologist at Mather had recommended. He'd made
an appointment with a Dr. Gee, who specialized in children's cancer.
Dr. Gee suggested admitting Sal for treatment, which he would discuss with us after he was in. Now, are you ready for this? I went to
admitting and showed them all my Screen Actors Guild insurance
documents (*thank God for them*). Well, they wouldn't admit him
unless I gave them a $10,000 deposit. I said, "Are you kidding me?
You have all my insurance info. Our son could be dying, and you want
a deposit?" I was pissed. I said, "If I give you a deposit, will you guarantee that our son will come home?" RoseAnn was getting nervous
and said to just give them a check and let's get back to Sal.

21

God Please, Wake Us up from This Horrible Dream

Dr. Gee informed us that Sal had lymphoblastic leukemia and he was going to start him on a protocol of chemotherapy. After some trial and error with different protocols, they finally came up with something that brought his blood counts back close to normal. Ro and I were sleeping on the floor night after night, waiting to hear some good news.

Forty days later, Dr. Gee came in and said, "It looks like Sal is going into remission." "What does that mean—is he cured?" I asked. "No—it just means that the chemo is working to kill some of the leukemia, and it seems to be dissipating."

Sal still had to stay at Sloan Kettering to be closely monitored, so we decided to go home every night from then on, and return to the hospital each following morning. Our son was getting better, though. He'd made some friends who were going through the same thing as he was. He was making them laugh and telling them, "Everything will be all right." He was building up their morale.

But the chemo made him very sick, and it was horrible to watch him continually throw up in pain. He was a strong boy, though, and he put on a good front—so much that he suggested I go back to work and make people laugh. "I'll act as your manager and take calls from here," he said. So there he was, suffering, not knowing whether he was going to live or die, and he was taking calls every day from agents and keeping a book to put my dates in.

At times, he couldn't take the pain and the daily vomiting, so someone mentioned that marijuana helped with such side effects of chemo. Well, where the hell was I going to get that? After all, it's not like you can get a prescription for pot. I'd never used any, but I knew people who had, so I approached someone about it, and he was able to get some for us. Meanwhile, I asked Dr. Gee what he thought, and he said that it had been done before. So now I'm supplying my son with something I'd always been so opposed to, but we figured we'd do anything to ease his pain. He was frightened to try it at first. He didn't even know how to hold it, and neither did we, but we learned quickly—and sure enough, it helped. Thank God for the friend who gave us the stuff.

As time went by, Sal was getting better and better, and eventually it was time for him to come home—even though he still had to continue the chemo regimen. I decided to pick him up in a limo on the day he was to leave the hospital, so I hired someone I knew to pick him up. Of course, I went along. RoseAnn, meanwhile, stayed home to prepare a big pot of pasta with Italian sauce and sausages, meatballs—and beef *brocciole,* Sal's favorite.

He started to vomit fiercely on the way home, due to the chemo treatment he'd received before leaving. But we were prepared. The driver had brought along some bags and a pan, because I'd explained to him that this might happen. Poor Sal threw up most of the way home, but about twenty minutes before we arrived, he settled down and was feeling better. When we pulled into the driveway, RoseAnn and Guy were looking out the picture window and saw us. They both ran out to greet Sal, and the tears started to flow. We didn't expect this day to happen, but it did.

As we walked in the house, Sal took a deep breath and smelled the food on the stove—and with a big grin on his face, he said, "I'm home, Mom." From that day on, it was a constant vigil to make sure everything was going well. We had to go to Sloan Kettering five days a week for treatment the first month. After that, treatments were down to three a week—and then, just one. These last we were able to do at an oncology center in Smithtown, which was not far from home. Then we would periodically go back to see Dr. Gee for checkups, and everything was still good—Sal Jr. was still in remission.

Sal was in his senior year in high school and wanted to graduate. But when he went back to the school, they advised us that he'd missed too many days and tests, and that he shouldn't return just yet, as it would be difficult for him to graduate that year. Well, they had no idea who they were dealing with. My wife and I and Guy got a bunch of friends together, and we picketed the school for days. Then some of his classmates joined in and refused to attend school unless they reinstated him. The *Daily News* and *Newsday* picked up the story, as did Channel 12 News.

We wanted Sal back in school, and they'd fought us—but in the end, we won. They agreed to take him back. Sal didn't go back to school right away, though—he was still getting chemo treatments, and he didn't want to be embarrassed by throwing up in class. Instead we decided to get him some tutoring, so he could catch up at home.

22

The Brown's Hotel Incident, 1981

It was Labor Day weekend, 1981. I was booked at Brown's Hotel in Loch Sheldrake, New York, where I had appeared many times in the past. I knew the band very well, and I usually talked over my music with them before the show. On this occasion I had a new orchestration written for me by my conductor, Sal Sicari. I was opening in Vegas in two days, and I'd never done the chart before, so I needed a played rehearsal to learn the tempos.

Sal went to the theatre to rehearse the band, and when I arrived to do a sound check, Sal said, "There's a problem."

"What problem?" I asked.

He told me that one of the band members was upset that he had to rehearse. I asked him who it was. He told me, "The drummer." That was Joe Anello. I'd known him for years, so I approached him and ask what the problem was.

"Why the hell do we have to rehearse your shit?" he said. "We've done your act before."

I said, "Hey—it's a new chart. I need to have it played. You guys never did this one before."

He was very annoyed, and I don't know why because the band members got paid for their time. So why the big problem?

But the guy got belligerent with me and started off on a rant. I gestured to him by putting my hands in front of me at shoulder height and said, "I don't need this shit at this time in my life." I was thinking about Sal Junior, who was dealing with leukemia, and I felt this was trivial. Apparently he didn't. He pushed my hand away and shoved me against the backstage wall.

I took this as a threat, so as I leaned away from the wall, I came back with a right hook and punched him in the face, then a left hook to his eye. After that, I ran into my dressing room and stood in a corner so no one could get behind me. Then the band members came in, and I thought they were going to attack me, so I picked up a chair and smashed it on the floor. It broke off a leg, and I said, "Anyone comes near me, they get this."

Suddenly a few other people came in and broke it all up. Then Mrs. Brown came in and asked me what happened. I told her, then said, "I'm too upset to do the show. Let Joanne do the whole show." Joanne Engle was the opening act.

Mrs. Brown said, "You can't do that—we have a full house here to see you." The agent, Arnold Graham, called and talked to me for a while. I calmed down and said I'd do the show.

As I was changing for the show, the drummer walked by. I noticed his shirt was all bloody, so I offered him one of mine to wear, thinking it would be an act of peace. But he completely ignored me.

So I did the show, and the band—including the drummer—played the music. Of course, they had to—that's what they were paid for. After I finished my closing number, which happened to be "My Way," I headed for the curtain that concealed the backstage area. Once I was in the wings, emcee Bernie Miller called me back for another bow. But when I headed back to the stage, I was handcuffed by the South Fallsburg Police. I stuck my head through the curtain and said, "Bernie I'd like to come back out, but I'm a little tied up at the moment."

23

The Arrest

I was taken in a squad car to the police station, where they were ready to fingerprint and book me for assault. On this particular night I had a double show—I was to be at the Raleigh for a late show at one. Arnold Graham heard about the arrest and came to the station in his pajamas to find out what was going on. He was well known by the local cops, and he told them that I had 1,000 people waiting for me at the Raleigh Hotel. The officer said, "There's nothing we can do about that."

Arnold said, "Hold me as hostage until he does his show, and then you can bring him back." The cops all laughed at him, then I thought, *Wait a minute—he hit me first,* so I told the officer that I wanted to press charges against the drummer, and that I had just been defending myself.

The policeman walked into the other room and explained to the drummer what was going on. The guy freaked out and said, "Are you kidding?"

The cop said, "Nope."

As it turned out, the guy didn't want to be arrested, so we were both released. I went to the Raleigh, Arnold went home and back to bed, and the drummer went home dejected, and with a black eye.

Incidentally, the bastard sued me for $100,000, and a few years later, in 1984, with my mind totally on Sal Junior, I had to go to the court in Monticello, New York, with my witness Sal Sicari. In his opening statements to the jury, Joe Anello's lawyer stood next to me as I was seated at the defendant's table. Pointing at me and treating me as if I was on trial for murder, he brought up the incident with singer Helen Reddy. My lawyer objected to that, and the objection was sustained by the judge. The drummer's lawyer was a pompous ass who was trying to impress the jury. I guess he'd watched too many episodes of *Perry Mason.*

When Sal Sicari got on the stand, my lawyer asked him to explain in his own words what he had witnessed. When the plaintiff's lawyer heard that, he asked for a recess. The jury was dismissed, and he tried to get me to agree to a settlement of $50,000. I refused, and after two hours, I got him down to $1,500. See, I had a counter-claim for $100,000 in lost wages, because I didn't work at Brown's for over two years. I settled for the $1,500 only because I'd had enough. I wanted to get back to Sal Junior. I asked the judge for time to pay it, because of the circumstances back home. He gave me a year—another black eye for the drummer. I could have paid him that moment, but his lawyer had put me through hell. I dropped my counter-claim, which I'd only filed as a deterrent.

24

Back to School and on to Vegas

Back at home, Sal Junior was getting better, and after a few weeks of tutoring he went back to school. He studied real hard and was put on the list of graduates. Oh—by the way, he was completely bald, having lost all his hair because of the chemo. But he didn't care. "Hey—I'm alive," he said. "My hair will grow back." On graduation day, we were all there, and when Sal was called up to get his diploma, he walked proudly to the podium. He accepted his diploma with a beautiful smile on his face, and his fellow graduates gave him a standing ovation that lasted for a couple of minutes.

You want to talk about proud? What a day it was for all of us—something we'll never forget. The following school year, he was accepted into Suffolk Community College, where he majored in drama. He'd decided he wanted to be behind the scenes as a producer/director, so he studied stage set ups, techniques, lighting, and so on.

At last things were going along fine again. Sal met and fell in love with a beautiful girl named Barbara Catalano, and they planned to get married. Ro and I were so happy for both of them. I was back making people laugh around the country.

One day I got a call from a friend of mine, his name was Big Julie. He ran gambling junkets to the Dunes Hotel in Las Vegas. He said "I have a big junket going to the Dunes on Fourth of July weekend. We are honoring Joe DiMaggio, and we'd like you to come and do a show for us."

He also told me there would be no pay, but a great opportunity to work Vegas.

"I'll call you right back," I said. I had two bookings that weekend and thought about which was more important. It didn't take me long, I called the Rapp agency and begged off the scheduled dates, and then called Sal Sicari, my conductor at that time, and told him the Catskills were out and Vegas was in.

"What are you talking about," he asked.

I explained the situation to him and then called Big Julie back. But when I spoke to Julie I said, "I got out of my other dates, but please guarantee me that the owners and the entertainment director will be at my show." He assured me that would happen.

Once in Vegas, I met the entertainment director Jerry Conte and told him who I was. I then asked him what time my rehearsal was scheduled for. He acted as if he ha no idea what I was talking about, and I had to remind him of why I was there.

He said, "I have nothing to do with Big Julie's shows; you have to speak to him."

I spoke to Julie, he spoke to Jerry, and everything was set up. The night of the show, the audience was packed with guests and celebrities, including Telly Savalas, Kevin Dobson, Joe Di Maggio, and many sport figures.

Halfway through my show, Jerry Conte, the guy who had been obstinate with me, walked on stage.

I looked at Sal Sicari and said, "I think we're done at the Dunes." Jerry stopped my show for a moment and announced to the audience filled with high rollers (they were paying the bills) who were laughing their asses off, "Ladies and Gentlemen, I am sitting with Mr. and Mrs. Arthur Shanker, the owners of the Dunes. They want me to inform you that although Sal Richards has never appeared here before, it won't be long before you see his name on our marquee." The crowd applauded thunderously, I was dumfounded, Sal Sicari was grinning from ear to ear, and I thought to myself *Big Julie came through.*

Well I wound up opening the Dunes two weeks later at The Top of The Dunes, a small but great nightclub on the top floor of the hotel. I worked there on and off for two years. The great singer, Robert Goulet, was working downstairs in the main showroom and would come up and see my last show every night; we became good friends. Such good friends that he decided to bring me in the main showroom to open for him, what a ball that was. Robert was a fun guy and pulled some pranks on me while I was on stage, like rolling a golf ball across the stage and walking on with a golf club and saying "mind if I play through?" One time he even pedaled a bike across the stage without saying a word.

One night after I finished my show, I walked into my dressing room to change, but my pants and shirt were missing; the only thing left were my shoes and bathrobe. Of course I suspected that Goulet did it.

I waited for a serene moment in his act, walked on stage with my bathrobe on, my shoes in my hand and said, "I found my shoes, now were the hell are my pants and shirt?" Well he let out a burst of laughter, as did the audience. What fun! That's what it was all about, getting along and respecting each other. He is gone now, and I miss him, but I have a lot of great memories to fall back on.

While I was at the Dunes Hotel in Vegas, I sent for Sal, Guy, and RoseAnn, so they could spend time with me. They had a ball, and Sal was so thrilled to see my name on the marquee when he arrived that he burst into tears. He certainly was proud of his pop, but I was more proud of him for going through his ordeal and trying to live a normal life. From that point on, he became my road manager and made sure everything was okay with the gigs, sound, lights, rooms, etc.

I'll never forget when I got booked into the Golden Nugget in Atlantic City, in August 1982. I followed Jack Carter, and it was supposed to be a two-week run, but after one week the management approached me and asked if I'd like to stay longer. Of course I said yes, and it lasted six months. Sal was with me all the way, staying at the hotel and watching out for me.

Prior to that, I'd auditioned for a Woody Allen movie, *Broadway Danny Rose,* and I got the part. They said I'd be shooting in four weeks, and I figured that would work out great—two weeks at the Nugget, then the movie. Then I got a call from the production company right after I opened at the Nugget. They said my shooting dates were changed—"You'll have to shoot this week." But I'd just signed a contract for two weeks at the Nugget, and I wouldn't be able to do it. So I lost a Woody Allen movie, but gained six months at the Nugget. Two years later, I wound up headlining AC—and I still do. What a business!

I did a movie called *Fighting Back* with Tom Skerritt, a co-starring role in a film about crime in an Italian neighborhood of Philadelphia. Sal Junior took all his friends to see the movie, and then he went every day. That's how so proud he was. I'd done other movies and TV before, and I've done some since then too, but that's not what this story is really about.

Mom and Dad in their early years.

Mom and Dad's wedding day.

My biological father, PFC. John J. Giovia, three weeks before he was killed in action during WWII, in the Philippines, at age 33.

Party in Brooklyn in 1950. Mom and Dad on left, my brother Joe and I, bottom center.

Family photo.

Me, at age four, wearing my dad's army hat.

Me, age sixteen, during my boxing days.

J.H.S. 162 class show, 1952.

Honeymoon.

Guy, age 3 and Sal Jr., age 5.

DeKalb Avenue, Ridgewood, Brooklyn—where I fell from the window, 1944.
Photo credit Merlis/Brooklynpix.com

Me, Sal Jr., Guy, and Ro—graduation day.

Sal Jr. with his friend, heavyweight boxer, Gerry Cooney.

Autograph to Sal Jr. from Frank Sinatra.

My boys and me.

My mom and Sal Jr., one year before passing on.

Guy and the dancers, John and Damien, from our Broadway show.

The Royal-Aires
Gallo Recording Artists

The Royal-Aires.

My band—The Club Daters, 1968.

My restaurant in West Palm Beach, Florida.

RoseAnn and me, with Buddy Greco, Connie Stevens, and our staff.

Buddy Greco, bartender, me, and maitre d'—LaMaganette Night Club, NYC.

Induction to the Celebrity Path—Brooklyn Botanical Gardens.

Ro and me waiting for the next gondola in Venice, Italy, 1998.

Billboard—Atlantic City 2001.

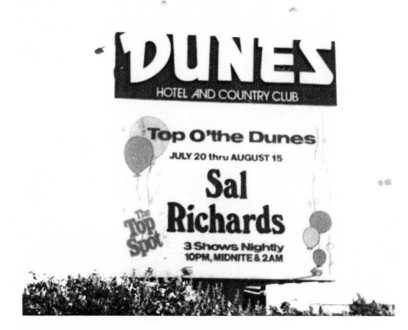

Billboard—Dunes Hotel in Vegas, 1981.

Joy Behar and Bobby Alto performing at a party at our house.

Sal Sicari, me and Father Frank—cutting the "Going to Vegas Cake."

Aliza Kashi, me, and Red Buttons.

RoseAnn, Jay Leno, and me at Fundraiser Trump Mara Lago, Palm Beach, Florida.

Muhammad Ali makes me laugh, along with the owner of the Dunes in Las Vegas, and Robert Goulet.

What a thrill meeting Perry Como.

Golfing with Micky Mantle.

Me and my idol, Sid Caesar.

Hanging with Milton Berle.

Ben Stiller and me at the NY Alumni Show.

My friend,Tony Orlando, and me, after a show.

Ro and me with Marty Allen and Katie Blackwell.

Performing with Rita Moreno in Los Angeles.

Having fun with Al Martino after dinner at his home.

Connie Stevens, Fran Zigman, Lainie Kazan, Rene Taylor, Sammy Shore, Joe Bologna, and me—after a show for the NY Alumni in Beverly Hills, CA.

Soupy Sales emcees a roast for me at the Tropicana in Atlantic City, celebrating forty years in show business, 1999.

Comedian, Shecky Greene, roasts me at my 70th birthday party.

My son, Guy, joins the roast.

Ro and me enjoying the roast.

Of course, I got the last word.

Celebrating their success in the Best Docmentary Feature category are Greg Principato, left, holding the award, RoseAnn Richards, Sal Richards, and their son, Guy Richards.

Ro and Sal on their wedding day.

Michael Imperioli, Tony Sirico, Sal Richards, and Steve Shirippa after a Soprano's Show in Michigan.

Guy, Sal Jr., and me at his graduation party.

My friend, Joy Behar, of "The View," and me at a screening of my Documentary at the Friars Club in New York.

Sal Jr. with Dr.Gee and his family.

Robert Goulet hid my clothes backstage—I walked on stage while he was singing and said, "I found my shoes, where are my pants?"

Sal and RoseAnn with their dear friend, Connie Francis.

Guy meets his son, Joseph, for the first time.

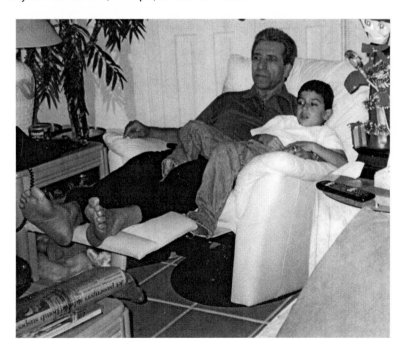

Enjoying time with my grandson, Joseph.

Al Martino, Frankie Valle, Jerry Vale, Perry Como, me, and Pat Cooper at a Bocce Tournament in Atlantic City, 1986.

Me and my friend, Yankee first baseman Joe Pepitone, at a fundraiser in 1992.

Producer Jules Nasso, Jerry Strivelli, Steven Segal, Ronnie Mascone, and me—set of "Out For Justice" in 1991.

John Lem, Rudy Gasparik, Frank Amodeo, and me—The Royal-Aires rehearsing in 1957.

Marlon Brando, Al Martino,Robert Duval, and me (sitting) in "The Godfather,"
1971.

Me, Rita Moreno, Gloria Loring, Fred Travalena, Donald O'Conner and
Peter Allen on stage at the Claridge in AC—New Years Eve, 1985.

Sal Jr. and James Woods on the set of "And Your Name Is Jonah," 1977.

Sal and son Guy performing together in Atlantic City.

25

Are We a Family Again?

By 1983, things were somewhat normal again. Sal was still in remission, still going out with Barbara. Guy was doing his thing in school, doing what he loved—playing football and riding motocross. He was rough-and-tumble as a kid, with a solid heart and a strong love for his brother. They used to make videos for me to watch when I came home from a gig. I laughed till it hurt, that's how funny they were together. RoseAnn and I were catching up on some lost moments, but it didn't last long.

Fast forward to Christmas week, 1983, when I had to go out of town for three days. Sal Junior had a cold, and as I was preparing to leave, he was complaining about having difficulty breathing. Ro said to me, "I'll take him to the hospital and get him checked. You go to work." I called her from where I was and asked how Sal was doing. She told me that they were going to give him some antibiotics and send him home. I got back on Christmas day and Sal was still having trouble, so we took him back to the hospital. The doctor suggested that they admit him for observation. Sal was very upset with that and said, "I'm not staying. It's my birthday tomorrow. I'm not going to be in a hospital on my birthday again." We couldn't convince him to stay, so the doctor prescribed another antibiotic—Keflex.

So we went home, but two days later, Sal was back in the hospital—this time St. Charles Hospital in Port Jefferson. He was coughing and running a fever. By New Year's Eve day, the nurse told us that she couldn't keep a constant eye on Sal on the floor he was on and suggested he be moved to ICU. We agreed and she called Dr. Fox. When we heard her arguing with him, I grabbed the phone and told him that this had to be done.

He said, "You're overreacting."

I said, "I'm paying for this, not you. I want you to write orders to move him."

The doctor agreed and Sal was put into intensive care. Seeing that it was New Year's Eve by now, RoseAnn had Dr. Fox write a note saying that she could stay with him until I got back from my show. Before I left, I asked Sal if he wanted me to stay. I told him I could get someone to fill in for me. He just said, "No, Dad—you go make 'em laugh. I'll be okay." As I was about to leave, I told Sal how much I loved him. He looked at me and said, "I love you too, Dad." Damn, I hated to leave.

Anyway, I was off to do my show. Our friends Dave and Lynette had been with us at the hospital, so Lynette stayed with Ro, and Dave drove me to work. When I got to my gig, I called RoseAnn. "So far, so good," she told me. I said, "I'll meet you at the hospital, but first I'll drop off my clothes and music at home. It's on the way."

I finished my show at 12:10, hopped in the car, and headed back home. When I got to the house, RoseAnn and Lynette were sitting in the kitchen. "What are you doing here?" I asked Ro. She told me that the nurses had thrown her out of ICU—they didn't care about the note from the doctor. "Sal was getting very upset because he heard the nurses telling me to leave. Then they called security, so we left."

We decided to call to see how he was doing, and they told us everything was fine. When I asked Ro if she wanted to go back, she said that Sal was upset and she thought it would be best for him to just rest. So we said goodnight to Dave and Lynette, and when they left, we went to bed.

26

Please Tell Me This Is a Nightmare

At 7:00 A.M., January 1, 1984, the phone rang. It was the doctor. I asked what was wrong, and he told me that Sal had adult respiratory distress syndrome, but they had it under control. I told him that we'd be right there.

We went straight to Sal's room when got to the hospital, and when we saw him, we thought, *Oh my God, what happened to our son?* His eyes were rolled back in his head, his mouth was all distorted, his hands were curled backwards, and he was on a respirator. What the fuck was this all about? They'd said it was under control. Where was that lying idiot, Dr. Fox?

RoseAnn and I were in a panic, not knowing which way to turn, or who to ask for help. Our son was in a *coma?* He'd lost oxygen to the brain? They'd had to paddle him three times because his heart had stopped? What was this all about? Why? Who'd done this? And what was this about a bad reaction to his medications? This was the ICU. Where were the nurses? Why was the man in his room moved? Something wasn't right. I was going to kill somebody. My poor RoseAnn was hysterical, gripping Sal's hand, calling to him. "Please no, no...this can't be happening. Why, God, why? He was doing so well."

They told us he was brain dead, that he had no chance of surviving. But we wouldn't accept it, and as we go on, you'll read about what we went through over the next ten months, trying to bring our son out of his coma. Right now, though, I'm getting too emotional to continue— writing this has brought it all back to me. We'll meet in the next chapter.

27

Dear Lord, Please Help Our Son

We stayed at the hospital all night, going back and forth to Sal's room to check on him and, hopefully, to see some signs of life. But we saw only agony and distress. My wife's cousins, Dorothy and Tessie were there—they'd come to the hospital to give us comfort. I couldn't sleep, but that was probably because of the coffee I was drinking to stay awake. So they slipped a Valium into my coffee, and that put me out cold.

By the time I woke up, family had started to arrive: my mother, father, brothers and sister, Ro's brother and his wife, and her mom and dad—who'd flown up from Florida. They had no idea what had happened or what they were about to see. We tried to ease some of the pain by explaining the situation, but they were anxious to see Sal and didn't hear much of what we said.

As they walked into the room and saw Sal's condition, their eyes went wide with astonishment when they realized what they were seeing. The tears flowed like rain from everyone's eyes. We escorted them to a room down the hall, and then explained everything again. Needless to say, they were all in shock, and then the questions started: "Is he going to die?" "Why did this happen?" We couldn't answer any of their questions because we didn't *have* the answers.

Days went by, and then weeks, and there were still no answers. So we contacted the Coma Arousal Center in Roosevelt, Long Island, and spoke with a Dr. Mihai Dimancescu, the head neurologist at that hospital. He came to examine Sal and showed us a program to stimulate the five senses.

We gave that a shot, and it started to work. Sal's body was almost back to normal—he was breathing on a respirator and starting to look as normal as anyone in a coma could look. But we found hope in that. With elements of the program being done all day long at fifteen-minute intervals, Sal started to respond, moving his arm and fingers on command. When we put certain bits of food in his mouth, he reacted to the taste. Lemon made him grimace, while sweets got a better reaction. When he got a taste of his mom's sauce, we could see a very strong response. He would move his tongue around in his mouth as if he wanted more.

We informed the nurses and doctors that he was starting to respond, and when the nurses watched they saw the movements we were seeing. They informed the neurosurgeons on the case and charted everything they saw.

28

The Doctors

The two doctors on the case came into the room, and one of them said, "I hear he's responding."

"Yes he is," I said.

They wanted us to show them, so RoseAnn did the same thing she did every day—she sat on the side of the bed and told Sal, "I'm here, Sal. It's Mom. Turn your head and look at me."

He'd responded every single day, but on this day, he didn't. The doctors said, "You're wasting your time. There's no hope for your son." RoseAnn kept begging Sal to turn his head, but he didn't do it. Then we saw something we saw often before he went into the coma. When something angered him, he would snarl, his lip would rise, and we would know he was angry.

Sal did this and we said to the doctors, "Did you see that?"

They said they did, but insisted it was a reflexive movement.

I said, "No—he's angry about what you're saying, and he's show-ing it. It's in God's hands."

One doctor threw up his hands and said, "God's hands? You folks are dreamers."

I stood up and asked RoseAnn to stop trying to get him to turn his head. Then I told these bastards to leave and never come back. I fired them. "Don't ever go near our son again," I said. Their jaws dropped, and they looked at me like I was crazy. "Don't test me because you could wind up like my son," I shouted again. "DON'T COME BACK!"

Ro and I continued to do what was necessary to try to wake our son, and for a while things were going well. Sal was off the respirator, breathing on his own with the help of an oxygen mask. His vitals were good, and the leukemia was still in remission. But one day, when we arrived and got ready to start our day, we saw that Sal was back on a respirator. We immediately asked why, and were told that he wasn't getting enough oxygen from the mask.

We wanted to know why. "What happened since last night?" I asked. One of the nurses came over to us and told us in confidence that someone had switched the oxygen tube with the suction machine, and rather than providing oxygen, the machine was drawing it out. After that, we never saw that nurse again. So now we were back to getting him off the respirator once again.

There were nights when we would get a call from St. Charles Hospital at about ten, saying the nurse in charge of Sal had called in sick and they had no one to watch him. So my wife and I would go to the hospital and cover the nurse's eight-hour shift. We'd learned how to suction and do other things prior to this, so we were ready. This happened so often that we started to think they were screwing around with us. I spent many nights taking care of Sal because the nurse did not show. It was bullshit. What if I fucked up? Would they take over for me? I didn't think so, so I hired our own nurse to cover the shifts when they had a problem.

We went down to the administrator's office to discuss all of this, and he suggested that perhaps we'd done something to end our son's dilemma.

"Are you out of your mind?" I said. I was really steamed. "You're accusing us of trying to kill our *son?* Someone on your staff made a mistake, and you're blaming us? It's easy for you to sit in that chair and say what you want, when you know that your people did something wrong on New Year's Eve to cause all of this. And what about your nurses not showing up to take care of him?"

He said to me in a condescending way, "Would you like to sit here?"

I told him no, but the day would come when he'd be sitting in a chair and telling the truth.

We immediately call Dr. Dimancescu and told him about what was going on, and how Sal was starting to respond. He came to St. Charles Hospital, examined Sal, and said he was a candidate for the arousal program at his hospital.

29

Off to the Coma Arousal Center

Sal was admitted to the center and, under the supervision of Dr. Dimancescu and his nurse associate, Robin Grass, they started working with him immediately. The compassion they had for family was unbelievable—they showed love and feelings for everyone. Any time we had a question, they didn't hesitate to answer. Robin was an angel from heaven, giving us hope every day. She worked with us, and comforted us as we worked with Sal. It made us feel much better to be there and away from St. Charles Hospital.

About a month later, they told us that it would be okay to discharge Sal. They suggested we look for a good nursing home, a place where we could continue with the program. We searched high and low, visiting many nursing homes and rehab facilities, but they were all filled with elderly people. We just felt he wouldn't get the care necessary for his treatment in places like that, so we asked if the hospital could keep him for a little while longer. We had a plan.

I called my cousin, Peter Massaro, who was a builder, and told him of my problem. I asked if he could convert my garage into the equivalent of a hospital room. His simply said, "It's done—we'll start tomorrow." What a gracious gesture. He finished in two days, and when I asked how much, he said, "It's my gift to you and Ro—and, of course, Sal Junior." Well, what a room it was, stocked with hospital supplies, an oxygen machine, a suction machine, a respirator if needed—and my insurance covered all of the equipment and nursing care twenty-four hours a day. My thanks to the Screen Actors Guild for the coverage, and thank you, Peter, for your loving ways.

30

Home Sweet Home

Holy shit—who would've believed that we'd wind up caring for our son in our own house? But at least we'd finally be able to give some attention to Guy, who'd also been suffering through all of this. Anyway, here we were, all back home, Ro doing some cooking again, Guy going to school, me getting back to work, family and friends helping out with the program. This would start at 8:00 A.M. and end at 10:00 P.M. every day. We set up a TV in Sal's room and put on some of his favorite shows daily—comedies, usually. We'd play music all day, read the paper to him, and watch for his responses. Dr. Morton Jagust, our good friend, came by once a week to check his vitals and confer with the nurses. He saw some of Sal's reactions and was very pleased. He told us to keep the faith.

It was difficult going back to making people laugh while my son was in a coma. What the fuck was funny about that? But that was all I knew, and I was running out of money. We had the insurance, but there were still many expenses that were not covered—and on top of everything else, I owed the IRS money. So it was back to work, as hard as it was. I'd finish a show, then go backstage and punch a hole in the wall. I missed my son being there with me, and I wondered if I could go on.

Well, with the help of my strong and beautiful wife, I continued—and things were going along fine until an IRS guy came to my door. When I let him in, he asked why I hadn't responded to the letters about my delinquent taxes. I tried to explain that my son has been sick and it had been rough. He said that was no excuse that the taxes were owed from last year. That's when I had enough. I asked him to follow me and showed him Sal's room. There he saw the equipment, the nurse, and the young man in the bed. I said, "This is my son. He's been in a coma for five months. If you can wake him up, I'll pay the taxes. Now get out of my house!" He left without saying a word. I eventually paid the taxes, but it was a year later, and I got them to waive the interest and the penalties.

I got a call to do an episode of the TV series *Matt Houston,* and when I told Sal, he reacted with a hint of a smile. So I knew he was still in there, but he couldn't come out yet. Anyway, I flew out to California, met with the producers, and shot the episode. It may have seemed exciting, but I couldn't sleep at night. I was constantly on the phone with RoseAnn, to check on how Sal was doing and to make sure she and Guy were okay. With great love and understanding, she assured me that everything was fine, and told me just to do a good job and not worry. It was easy for her to say, but hard for me to hear. I felt like I shouldn't be away from home, but since this was what I did for a living, I had to do it through the pain.

A few days later, I finished the shoot and headed back home. I was happy about that and couldn't wait to get back to my family.

31

Back Home Again

Now things were starting to get a little better as Ro and I continued with the Coma Arousal Center's program. I was working more, and we had help from family and friends. Every so often, the nurses insisted that we get out for a while, so we would take Guy to dinner and the movies, just to relieve the strain for a few hours. It felt good, but once we got home it was back to reality.

It was now July 1984, and things were going along as usual. My mother was coming over every day to help out with Sal. She'd rub his feet, pray, and cry constantly. He was her first grandchild, and we could see her pain. One night, our nurse, Karen, noticed that Sal was having a problem breathing and suggested we transport him back to the hospital as a precautionary measure. So we called for an ambulance and took him back to St. Charles, because that's where all his records were kept. They settled him in, put him back on a respirator, and he gradually got a little better. Our mothers came over to the hospital in a panic, thinking the worst, but we told them it was for a checkup that couldn't be done at home.

That week I had a gig in Atlantic City, opening for Al Martino. Opening night went fine, and afterward I checked in with Ro as usual. She said, "He's fine—how was your show?"

I said, "It went great, but..."

She said, "No buts. Just keep up the good work." Boy, was she my ROCK!

That night, I went to dinner with Al and my manger at the time, Larry Spellman. After dinner, we sat around and reminisced about the business until about 1:00 A.M. I went to my room and noticed the message light blinking on the phone. Shaking all over, I picked it up to retrieve the message. *Could this be* the *call about Sal Junior? Is he gone?* I was scared shitless. I listened to the message, and it was from my brother-in-law, Tommy, telling me to call ASAP, that there was a problem. I sank into the chair. I didn't want to call. I didn't want to hear that Sal had died. I called Larry and asked him to come to my room. He came right away. I told him what was going on and asked him to stay with me for support.

"Of course," he said. "Take it easy, Sal—make the call and find out. Maybe it's not that serious."

I made the call, and the first thing I said was, "What's going on with my son?"

"Calm down," said Tommy. "He's having a slight problem, but they have it under control. Ro and Denise are with him. It's your mother."

"What's wrong with my mother?" I asked.

He told me that she'd had an aneurysm and was in Stony Brook Hospital. "Your dad wants you to call the waiting area so he can talk to you." I called as soon as he gave me the number. The whole family was there. Since Dad was too distraught to speak to me, my brother Steve got on the phone and told me that Mom was in a coma. *Oh my God,* I thought, *what the fuck is happening to this family? No—this can't be true. She's only sixty-four. Not Mom...please.*

32

Two Loved Ones in a Coma

I told Larry that I had to get home now, so he checked with the transportation desk and they said they could have a car ready in an hour. It was now 2:00 A.M. It would be five hours before I got back to Long Island. I wanted to go now, so I woke up one of the hotel executives and told him my dilemma. He told me he knew a guy with a private plane at Bader Field. He called him, and the guy agreed to fly me home, but it was going to cost me $700. I said, "Get him now—I don't care about the money." I was at Bader Field within twenty minutes. The plane was ready and I was off, and forty-five minutes later, I was at Islip Airport. I jumped in a cab and went to see Sal Junior first at St. Charles. When I arrived, I found Ro and Denise sleeping in the bed next to Sal's. I woke them, and Ro was shocked to see me. She got up, hugged me tight, and said, "We're okay here. Go see your mother. I'll explain about Sal later."

I found our car in the parking lot and drove to Stony Brook Hospital. When I got to Mom's floor, I was met by Steven, Joey, and Debbie, my brothers and sister. They explained everything to me. I went to Mom's room and found Dad holding her hand and talking feverishly, trying to get her to wake up. He saw me and started to cry. Then we all cried. I walked over to the bed and looked at my mother. She wasn't moving, her face was swollen, and tubes protruded from everywhere. *Oh no, this can't be happening,* I thought. I instinctively started doing things that I'd learned at the Coma Arousal Center, running a pencil up the bottom of her foot, down her arms, and on her hands, looking for any movement, but it was to no avail. I stayed with them all night.

Finally my dad said, "Go see your son—you can't do anything here."

I was hesitant to leave, but I was in an unfortunate predicament— Mom in one hospital and Sal in another. After a while, I decided to go, and when I arrived back at Sal's hospital, RoseAnn and Denise were up. Ro explained that something had been lodged in Sal's throat and they'd had to suction it out. It took awhile, but they got it and everything was fine now. How ironic for this to have happened on the same night that Mom took ill. They wanted to go and see Mom, so I stayed with Sal. When they returned, it was clear that there'd been no improvement. They told me the neurosurgeon was going to see her, and that we should go back to hear what he had to say.

33

Back with Mom and the Family

As I approached the family, I could see by the look on their faces that things weren't looking too good. They told me that the doctors all agreed that she was brain dead. *Oh! God—where have I heard that before...it is starting all over again?* Now we had two cherished souls fighting for their lives. What to do next? With all we'd been through up to now, I figured I might have some answers. I told the family about Dr. Dimancescu and the Coma Arousal Program, but they were a little hesitant to respond.

Finally Dad said, "Why don't you go back to AC and finish your gig? We can talk about this when you come home." When I said it might be too late then, they all insisted that I go—including Rose-Ann. So I took a bus back to AC, reluctant to go on stage, but Larry said to me, "This is what you do, so do the best you can." I did the rest of the week, struggling through each show, still getting the laughs, but all the while thinking of Mom and Sal.

When I got back home, Mom was still the same. Over the next few days, Sal showed some improvement. Mom, on the other hand, was getting worse—no response at all. Then I got the call from my brother, Steve. "Mom is gone."

RoseAnn and I rushed over to my father's house. Everyone was there, and the tears were flowing. A vibrant, funny, and loving woman of sixty-four had been taken from us much too soon.

Now it was time to make funeral arrangements. We all agreed on a one-day viewing, so everyone could remember how she was without having to gawk at her in a casket for three days. Needless to say, hundreds of people came to pay their respects, and Father Frank gave a beautiful eulogy.

At the gravesite the next day, we all stood, stunned, not believing that this could have happened. Dad was a physical wreck and Debbie was heartbroken. We three brothers—Steve, Joey, and I—tried to appear strong on the outside for the family's sake, but on the inside we were falling apart. We all went back to Dad's house and sat around reminiscing about Mom, hurting—and at times, laughing at some of the things she used to do to make people laugh. I guess that's where I got it from...my mother.

The next day I had to leave for South Carolina to do a movie called *Cat's Eye*. I was going to cancel, but again Ro said to me, "You have to go. You can't cancel now. This is what Mom and Sal would want you to do." So I went, did the movie, and came back three days later to continue grieving for Mom, and trying to wake Sal Junior.

34

Sal Says Goodbye and Goes to God

As time passed, although suffering the pain from the loss of my mother, we still had a project ahead of us. We had to get back to Sal Junior and try to wake him from his coma. Things went along as smooth as possible for a while; but there came a time when Sal was not responding to the coma arousal techniques we were administering. Some problems developed, so we called Dr. Dimancescu. After explaining what we were noticing, he suggested we take Sal into South Shore Hospital on Long Island. So we did that. We hired an ambulance company to transport Sal to the hospital for evaluation, and we went to see him every day. They were giving him blood tests and checking his vitals constantly. They did everything they possibly could do to find out what was going on. A few days later we got a call from the doctor, and he asked us to come to the hospital. Of course, RoseAnn and I were afraid for our son. We couldn't understand what was going on—we just didn't know. So we went to the hospital and saw Dr. Dimancescu, and he gave us some terrible news. He told us that Sal Junior's organs were starting to fail, and it was not because of the leukemia. There weren't any signs of leukemia in his body. He was still in remission. He told us his NG tube—the feeding tube— was starting to emit a gritty dark substance, which indicated that Sal was bleeding internally. Of course we asked how this could be happening. It was explained to us that because Sal had been in the coma and lying down for so long, not able to respond to treatment, that his organs could no longer function properly. The doctor didn't think he was going to last the day. What a cruel irony this was. Sal had beaten the leukemia—periodic blood tests during his coma confirmed that it was gone—and now he was going to die because of a bad reaction to a lousy drug?

So RoseAnn and I called the family, and a priest to administer last rites. Of course, we were all there, continuing to pray, hoping this was not true, waiting for a miracle to happen. As we all stood around the bedside, I walked over to Sal and started talking to him. *We know you're in pain and that asking you to stay was selfish, asking you to hang on, hang on, hang on, not realizing the pain you were in, and you were probably doing it for us. But what I'd like to say to you right now is, if you see a light, and at the light you see a woman standing there with another man, know that they're your grandmother and grandfather waiting to take you to heaven. So go and grasp their hands and go with them to God.*

And then RoseAnn walked over and held his hand, which was down by his side. While she was holding his hand and sort of looking at him in the same way, sort of expressing the same feelings I was, we were all stunned because Sal suddenly took his mother's hand, grabbed it, and placed it up to his chest by his heart. It was as if he was saying goodbye, because as he held her hand there, his head went to the side—and then he was gone.

So now, of course, the family and everyone were in pain from seeing this happen, and we were praying. My wife and I had to speak to them, to give them the strength to understand what was going on, that he had been suffering for ten months in this coma. We did everything we possibly could do so he might survive but, unfortunately, it was his time. So I said, let's think about this. Maybe this was the miracle we've been praying for—to relieve Sal from his pain so he could go to heaven.

35

The Funeral

Now it was time to go home and prepare for the funeral, never thinking that we would ever have to bury our child. It was always supposed to be the other way around. We were supposed to go first, and our children were supposed to stay around to carry on. The wake was held at Giove Funeral Parlor in Selden, and over 500 people came. There were flowers all around the room, all around the casket, and even out into the hall. There were friends and family, agents, and show biz people, all coming to pay their respects. It was really a tribute to my son because everyone knew and loved him.

RoseAnn and I hired a motorcade of police officers on motorcycles to escort us to the church and cemetery. We did this because we knew it was something that Sal would like. The mass was held at Infant Jesus Church in Port Jefferson, and Father Frank presided over the mass. Father Frank and Sal were close, and Sal knew him very well because he spoke sometimes at Father Frank's Hope House Ministries to people dealing with drug addiction and substance abuse. Sal would say things like, "I'm on drugs right now. The drugs are to save my life. The drugs you are doing can kill you." During the mass, Father Frank said some wonderful, beautiful things about our son.

At the gravesite, more pain entered our hearts because Sal Junior was buried back-to-back with my mom. You could almost say on the same plot. Now we had to suffer through that with my brothers, my sister, my father, and the rest of the family, knowing that we were getting ready to bury Sal, and my mother was there, having died only four months earlier. It was a real difficult day. RoseAnn, my beloved wife, had the strength of a lion. She spoke to everyone at the gravesite—even with her broken heart. I don't know how she did it, but she said some beautiful, beautiful things, and made everyone there feel comfortable, asking them to accept what had happened as a miracle from God.

36

Why Should I Make People Laugh?

RoseAnn and I cried ourselves to sleep for months. I didn't want to work, but comedy was all I knew, and I needed to make some money. But I couldn't get myself to the point where I wanted to go and make people laugh. I figured with all that had happened, why should I make people laugh? They didn't deserve to laugh while I was suffering. But RoseAnn reminded me that those people didn't do this to me, so it wasn't something I should deprive them of. "They may be having problems, but when you make them laugh, you take their problems away for an hour or so. That's the gift that you were given and you have to project that."

My first gig after Sal's death was in upstate New York, in the Catskills. It was the hardest thing I ever had to do in my life. Standing backstage, I realized that in minutes I'd have to perform for people who had no idea what was going on, and I had to go out and act like nothing had happened to me. Well, I did it. It all came back to me. The show went terrific, but after I finished the show and went backstage, the pain was devastating. I was mad at myself. How could I do this? How could go out and have fun when I'd just buried my son?

When I got in the car, I cried all the way home. I just couldn't stop crying. RoseAnn had waited up for me, of course, and as she always did—but this time with a little more passion—she asked me how it went. I told her it had gone well. I did my show and did what I had to do. I made them laugh, and it was as if I had never left the stage. So now, I'd broken the barrier. I was back.

Here's the thing: every show I do, even now, I feel his presence—and I know I always will. It's like he never left, and he's always standing there, believing in me, patting me on the back and saying, "Have a good show, Dad."

37

The Visit

It was a little over a year since the passing of our son Sal Junior, my sister Deborah and her husband Joe came over to our house for coffee and cake. We were all sitting at the kitchen table talking and having coffee when RoseAnn excused herself to go to the bathroom. Over our kitchen table was a hanging lamp, for some reason I looked up during our conversation and I noticed the lamp swaying left to right like a pendulum. I asked my sister to look at the light and tell me what she saw, her and Joe both looked up and confirmed the movement. We looked at each other, puzzled as to why this light was swaying. It was a calm evening, there was no wind outside, and no doors were open. There was just stillness throughout the house.

As RoseAnn came back into the kitchen and before we could say anything to her, she said, "Look at the chandelier in the dining room. It is moving side to side."

The three of us looked at her in amazement and then looked into the dining room. Sure enough, the chandelier was swaying.

"Ro," I said. "Look at the kitchen lamp."

"What the hell is happening?" she asked, concerned. Both lamps were swaying the same way, side to side, in unison with each other.

I went to the front door to see if it was open; maybe a breeze was coming in. I checked all the windows in the living room. Everything was closed. As I walked into the living room, there was a hanging lamp over our television, and sure enough it was swaying the same way as the others. Now we are all getting nervous.

"What's going on?" I wondered out loud. Having an investigative mind, I called the police and asked if there was any form of ground disturbance in our area that could cause things to move. They said nothing had been reported. I then went outside to see if maybe a large truck had gone by to cause vibration; there was nothing. Even the trees were as still as could be, there wasn't even a breeze.

My brother-in-law, who is from Italy and does not speak English well, said to my sister, "I am frightened, I think the Diablo (devil) is here."

"Don't ever say the devil is in our home!" I screamed at him. "If you want to leave, go right ahead."

My sister insisted on staying, she wanted to see if we could find out what was causing this.

The whole time we were investigating, the lights continued swaying. Our son Guy was in the den, he had fallen asleep watching television. We went in to wake him so he could see this phenomenon, but as we walk into the den, which had a cathedral ceiling, we noticed that the large hanging lamp in the center was also swaying.

"Oh my God," RoseAnn said. "What is going on?"

We woke up Guy, and as he got up, he noticed the hanging lamp over the bar in the den also swaying. Now, every hanging lamp in the house was swaying so evenly and exactly in time with each other. It was bizarre.

Guy looked and then asked groggily, "What's going on? Why is the lamp moving over the bar?" We showed him all the other lamps that were moving; this was his take on the whole thing:

"Remember the poem Sal wrote about reaching the light? Well I hear you and Mom in your bedroom every night crying out to him to give us a sign. To tell us that he's okay." He paused for a minute and then said, "Sal was here and he touched the lights; this was his way of reaching out."

Just a he said that, all the lamps stopped swaying at once, except for one. The one in a corner of the living room hanging over a small shrine we made for Sal Junior kept up its gentle movement.

When my brother-in-law heard this, he wanted to get out of the house as fast as he could. My sister said to him, "We are witnessing a miracle; don't you go anywhere."

We all stood around the shrine, which was the Pieta, of the Virgin Mother holding Jesus in her arms. We all wondered why this lamp was still swaying.

"Mom, Dad," said Guy softly. "The Pieta was in his coffin, and you both wanted to take it home. That was the last place you saw Sal before the burial."

The lamp stopped swaying.

"He has reached his resting place," said RoseAnn. The tears started to flow. Someone asked what the time was.

"It's 12:26 P.M.," I said. Sal Junior was born on December 26. Was this a coincidence? I don't think so.

I was still a little skeptical and tried everything from running up and down the stairs, to running around the bedrooms upstairs to see if anything moved, if any of the lamps started swaying again. Nothing moved.

The next day we invited Father Frank Pizzerelli to our home and explained the whole thing. He listened so intensely and, when we were done, he said, "You were blessed. Sal Junior paid you a visit, all the lights swaying was his way of saying I have reached the light. You will never see anything like this again; be grateful that this happened to you."

We removed all the hanging lights and replaced them with stationary fixtures. And he was right we never saw anything like it again, except in our memories and our dreams.

On the following page is the original copy of the poem that Sal Jr. wrote in 1983, while undergoing treatment for leukemia.

6-14-83

UNDECIDED

Listen to what I have to say,
I need someone to hear the way I feel.
Because the way I feel is very real.
I feel like I'm a prisoner surrounded by no bars.
A dreamer trying to go very far.
I see my life waiting in the light.
But every time I see it, I begin to see night.
I have to stand up on my own and start to achieve
all alone, and make this worth the fight.
I'm living in a world to survive.
Fighting very hard to stay alive.
And I know some day I will look back and see,
what that fight meant to me.
It made me reach the light.
When I look around I realize I'm not alone.
I can always turn my way back home.
That's good to know, but watch me grow, and
make it on my own.
I was put through a big test.
But I didn't try all my best
to achieve what I believe in.
But it's not too late, to open that gate - that gate
that's been locked so long.
All this time it could have been opened for a song.
Repeat Twice -*I'm living in a world to survive.*
Fighting very hard to stay alive.
And I know some day I will look back and see,
what that fight meant to me to reach the light.
Now you've heard the way I feel,
and I believe you are very real.
You see I pray and tell you this every night,
and ask you to guide me to that light
Repeat Once -

Lyrics by: Salvatore Giovia, Jr.

38

The Claridge Casino

As it always does, life went on. One day I got a call from the entertainment buyers at the Claridge Casino Hotel in Atlantic City. They asked me if I would be interested in coming down and looking at a room they would like to turn into a lounge, where I could perform and do my act. I took the ride down and went to meet with Roger Wagner, who was the president of the hotel. They showed me a small cubbyhole right next to the elevators, but I didn't think it would be suitable. However, I still hadn't headlined in Atlantic City, and they were thinking of putting me on a four-week run. So it was tempting. I was thinking, *Okay. I'll have a steady gig here.*

In my negotiations with Mr. Wagner, we talked about enlarging the room a little and making it brighter—to make it look like a real lounge. At the time it was sort of a bar area with couches and arm chairs, and a small stage. I suggested a few things to turn it around and make it more like a nightclub, and he agreed to my ideas. He'd seen me work before, when I'd opened for the Lennon Sisters at the Claridge a few months earlier. He told me he liked what I did and that I would be good for this new thing they were planning. So he changed the room around and asked if I had pictures with celebrities. I did, and he put them up on the walls of the lounge. It had been known as the Bombay Lounge, but they agreed to change the name to The Celebrity Cabaret.

After the work was done, I opened there. I had an opening act, and changed the act every two weeks. I did that only because I wanted to make the lounge feel more like a theater, and I booked various opening acts during that four-week period.

After the first two weeks, the room started to really fill up. There were lines around the corner of the club to the elevators, people waiting to get into the room. There were maybe ninety-five seats, and it was always jammed packed. People even leaned over the railings, looking into the room to see the show. Mr. Wagner liked what he saw and asked if I would like to stay another four weeks.

Well, those four weeks turned into two months, and eventually I wound up working there two-and-a-half, maybe three years. I would come in for two months, take two months off, then come back. They eventually had to build a bigger room to accommodate the crowds—and I considered that quite an honor. They went up another level and built a room there. While they were building this room, they wanted me to continue to perform there, so they put me in the main showroom to do my act.

When the room was finally finished, we had a grand opening; and they asked me who I would like to have in as my opening act. I had a friend who was in the business for a long time, and I asked him if he would mind coming in with me and sharing the stage as a co-headliner in the new Celebrity Cabaret. That guy was Buddy Greco. He was known not only as a great singer, but as an excellent musician and pianist. We were together for the first eight weeks of the grand opening, and we became very close—good friends. After that, we always worked together. There was no more changing of the acts.

After a while, the Claridge decided that they wanted to put Buddy Greco in his own spot, where he would be the headliner and have his own opening act—which was well deserved. So I went back to booking my own opening acts again, from singers to doo-wop groups—anything to please the audience and give them something I knew they would like. It was very successful, and the room was packed every night, two shows a night. It went on like that for two-and-a-half years.

Unfortunately, however, I had been putting on this big façade. It had only been five or six months since my son's passing, and the pain was starting to get worse. So I started drinking. I would have one drink one night, two drinks the next night, and before I knew it I was drinking every night. Although it didn't affect me onstage—I was able to perform—it did affect me offstage. My anger was becoming very noticeable to people around me, but they had no idea what was bothering me. Why did this guy change all of a sudden? In addition to the drinking, I started to gamble, and while I was gambling, I was getting boisterous at the tables. It was just not me, but I didn't know it. The booze had taken me over.

One day I was approached by Mr. Wagner, who had become a very good friend of mine. We liked each other as buddies, but as president and CEO of the hotel, he had to do what was right for them—and also right for me. He said, "We are going to have to break the relationship for your own sake and ours, because you are going in the wrong direction. No matter how funny you are on stage, and how many people like it, at night after the shows, you become a different person entirely, and this news is getting back to me. I never thought I would have to tell you this, but you have to leave." So I was fired from the Claridge Hotel.

After I was fired, they tried to keep the room open with the same format, but the Celebrity Cabaret suddenly began its downfall. For whatever reason, people stopped showing up. I believe it proved that people were coming because of the acts we had working every night, and having fun. Not only that, celebrities who came into the room would come up on the stage and perform with me. It was one of those rooms where you didn't know who was going to show up—celebs like Dom DeLuise, Rita Moreno, Peter Allen, Jay Leno, just to name a few. They would come in to see my show, and I would ask them to come up on stage, and they would get up on stage. Man, did I blow a good thing! I'd really blown it. I'd probably still be there today if I hadn't screwed up.

I didn't work in Atlantic City again until 1989, because even though show business is big, in many ways it's like a small community. When something like that happens, everybody finds out about it. I was kind of barred from Atlantic City. No one would hire me.

I decided right then and there that I was going to stop drinking and gambling—and while I was at it, to stop smoking too. I was still working the nightclubs and theaters around the country, but I missed Atlantic City.

39

The Return to Atlantic City

Eventually I got a call from an agent, who asked me if I would be interested in working at the Showboat Hotel on a percentage door deal. I said, "Well listen, I've got to do something. I've got to get back there." So I went and spoke with Bucky Howard, the president and CEO. He knew me, knew my problems, and knew what happened. I told him if he saw me do something out of line, he should just show me the door and I'd leave. So he gave me a chance.

I did a six-week engagement there. Again we were packed every night; two shows a night, 300 people every show. At the end of my show on closing night, Bucky and his wife came on stage with the dancers and RoseAnn. They rolled out a big cake to celebrate closing night, which was quite a surprise for me. Bucky made a speech to the audience and said, "Ladies and gentlemen, we have had Sal Richards here for six weeks, and I don't know what you have heard in the past, but let me tell you something—this man is what you call a stand-up guy, and one of the most honest men that I have come across."

Back headlining at all the top casinos in AC, I got a call from Stephanie Nielson, entertainment director for the Trump Taj Mahal. She knew me from work I'd done at other Trump properties. I thought she was calling for me to headline the hotel, but she wanted to know if I would co-headline with Vic Damone—same money, equal billing, and all the amenities. I said, what the hell. I knew Vic—we were friends, and it would be fun.

So, opening day came, and I arrived early. I found out that Vic was rehearsing, so I went to the Xanadu Room to see him. He was happy to see me, and I was happy to see him. We exchanged some niceties and parted on good terms.

Now it was show time, and I was getting ready in my dressing room. Ro was there to support me, and as I headed to the stage, I saw Vic, and it was the usual, "Break a leg—have a good show."

I hit at 8:00 P.M. and did a half hour. The audience was great—they came to have a good time.

When I opened, I would usually close my show with a mention of the star. So I told an old joke, and included myself and Vic in the story. It got a great response. I said, "Thank you—you've been great. Good night."

As I walked off into the wings, Vic was waiting to go on. I said to him, "Great crowd," but he did not reply.

I returned with RoseAnn to my dressing room, changed, and had a cup of coffee and some snacks. Just relaxing waiting for the show to end, we were all going to hook up and go to the private room for some food and fun.

After the show ended, there was a knock on my door. It was Vic's road manager, telling me Vic wanted to see me. So Ro and I locked up my dressing room and walked down the hall to his. I knocked on the door and he opened it, and as Ro and I started to walk in he stopped us cold.

"What's up?" I asked.

He reached out his hand. But it wasn't to shake mine—it was to grab me and pull me close to him. Then he said, "Don't ever mention my name in your act again."

"Are you kidding?" I asked.

He said, "No, I'm not kidding." Then his grip got tighter and he said, "Got it?"

I pulled him toward me and my grip got tighter, too. I said, "Got it."

What the hell was his problem? Vic Damone, one of the best singers in the business, and he is worried about me? I thought we were friends. He was friendly with RoseAnn, too, and we'd sat and talked for hours at a time about Buddhism, which he was into. I even worked Italian festivals with him. So what the fuck did I do?

40

The Private Party

Afterward, Ro and I arrived at the private room, and we walked over to the table that was set for the show's cast and friends. Vic was not there yet. Someone at the table told us that all the seats were reserved. I said, "You're right—for us and Damone's friends." The person said no—it was just for Mr. Damone. So I went to the maître d', but he was totally confused. He decided to escort us to another table, and we had fun despite Mr. Damone's arrogant behavior.

The next night I got the silent treatment, so I said, "I can't let this get in the way of my performance." I went on and did better than the night before, because when something or someone tries to intimidate me, I get stronger.

After my show, Vic asked me "How were they?" when I got into the wings. He knew—he'd heard the laughs. Was he being a smart ass, or what? So I said, "They were great for me—you better get out before they leave." Was that cruel? Maybe, but I was pissed, and I did not want to deal with him anymore.

We haven't seen or spoken to each other since—but man, I wish I could sing like him!

I've opened for Tony Bennett, Robert Goulet, Susan Anton, Jerry Vale, Al Martino, and Eddie Fisher, to name just a few, and never had a problem with any of them—except for Engelbert, but I will leave it at that.

41

Florida, Broadway, and Guy's Problems

While living in Lake Grove, Long Island, in the home that Sal Junior basically grew up in, there were a lot of things coming back into our lives that reminded us of him. Friends came by—people who didn't know he'd died, stopping to ask us about him. That was getting to us, so we decided to move to Florida. But we had another reason to move. Our son, Guy, distraught and so hurt over the loss of his brother, got hooked up with some wrong people. The next thing you know, he had a substance abuse problem.

We didn't find out for a while. We knew there was something wrong, but we were too blind to see it at that time. I remember once that we didn't see him for three days. I was looking all over for him day and night. We did not hear from him, and we didn't know what to think. When he finally came home, he looked terrible, and he had no shoes on. He was just not the jock we knew from high school.

We found out he was addicted to cocaine, so we got him right into rehab. He didn't want to go, and they told us we couldn't force him, that he had to do it on his own. But we were too concerned. We'd already lost one son, and we would *not* lose another one. We put him in rehab, but after a few days he left the facility.

When this went on for a while, we decided to move to Florida. After we got there, the environment changed him a little bit. But then

135

it started up again and kept getting worse and worse. We were at our wits' ends, and we didn't know what to do with him. Anyone who has lost a son or daughter to addiction understands what we went through. It was the worst thing imaginable.

We reminded Guy that his brother took drugs to save his life, but he was taking drugs to kill himself. Nevertheless, he was in and out of twenty different rehabs. We were paying all kinds of money because he didn't have insurance. This went on for a few years.

Finally, though, he reached a point in his life where he started to straighten out a little bit. In 1993, I went back to New York to put together a show for Broadway called *Three from Brooklyn*. It was a story loosely based on three dancers from Brooklyn trying to make it in show business. We put the show together and lined up our investors. Guy, being very talented, was part of a group called the Circle Break Dancers. This was back when break dancing was very hip. So he choreographed with two other dancers in the show.

He did a marvelous job—fantastic! When the show opened, he got great reviews. "The dancers were abound with virility," the critics said. So I thought, *Here we go—a Broadway show getting Guy noticed.* My son could come out of this and maybe get something for himself to further his career. The producers provided us with an apartment on 51st Street and Broadway, and Guy had an apartment in the same building.

But one night Guy didn't show up. We were getting ready to go on—show time, fifteen minutes to curtain—and I had to put his understudy in the show. When Guy came back the next day, I asked him where he was last night. "Something happened," he said. "I wasn't feeling good."

"Guy, we were in your apartment. We had the apartment manager open the door. It was locked, you weren't there. We didn't know where you were." But my wife saw him, and she didn't tell me. She saw him across the street from the theater. It was wintertime, and he was standing in the cold, hovering and freezing, with no jacket on.

So I said to him, "You used drugs, didn't you? You're fired." I never thought I would be firing my son, but I saw him going through what I'd gone through at the Claridge. Like me, he was doing something to hurt his career. I decided that applying tough love now was very important, so I fired him from the show.

After that, everything collapsed. There was a bad snowstorm, and because of that, ticket sales fell. We couldn't raise any more money. We had to give the show up, even though it had been doing well. We had advance sales, but we had to close the show because we were not allowed to use the advance money—we had to return it. I wondered what else was going to happen. What else were we going to go through in our lives?

Guy continued to use for a while after that. In Florida he got into trouble with the law, and we had to get lawyers. What my wife and I went through was unbelievable.

42

Two Nights at San Quentin Prison

There came a time while Guy was living in California around 1999 when he started to abuse drugs again.

And the more he used, the more he got in trouble with the law—cocaine possession, acting under the influence of a controlled substance, etc. Whenever he had any confrontation with the police, he would clamp his hand onto whatever coke he had left as if his life depended on it, which it probably did. When the police would open his hand and find the cocaine, Guy would be arrested.

This happened on many occasions and eventually he was facing prison time. We hired a lawyer who was recommended by some friends I had in Los Angeles to represent Guy. The lawyer did a good job and plea-bargained the sentence down to two years in San Quentin Prison as a repeat offender. If Guy had gone to trial he could have gotten five years, which was a little harsh for a non-violent crime. He was not selling drugs, just foolishly using.

Ro and I thought *San Quentin? That's a place for hardened criminals. What is going to happen to him?* Well leave it to Guy, with his strong will and his faith in God, and being a very strong minded man, he will make it through this difficult time in his life.

San Quentin had a semi-pro baseball team, called SQ Giants, which was rostered by the inmates, Guy played center field. San

Quentin would play other semi-pro base ball teams such as, the Novato Knicks from Sacramento inside the fifty foot walls of the prison. Guy made the headlines in the press with pictures and interviews. Guy tried to make us feel like prison was a camp, so we wouldn't have to worry. But we knew it was all a mochismo front.

The prison had a policy to invite families from out of the state to come and visit. They would accommodate you with a small apartment on the grounds of the prison. The area was gated and surrounded with barbed wired. It included 12- by 6-foot outside walking area. The apartment had a small kitchen, two small bedrooms, and a small living room. We filled out an application, and a few months later we were on our way to San Quentin.

When we arrived to "check in," we were searched and they inspected the bags of food we were allowed to bring in. As we were driven through the complex, we noticed the tower guards with high-powered rifles in their hands, what a sight to behold, believe me.

We arrived at the apartment, and Guy is waiting behind the locked gate. We had not seen him in over a year and wondered what he would look like under these conditions. He had a big smile on his face and was happy to see us; he looked good. The guard unlocked the gate, and we went in. As we hugged and kissed our son, the gate was locked behind us, what a scary feeling. For two days this was our domain, under watch and Guy reporting by phone every four hours to the guard house and then step outside for the guards to have a visual on my son at gun point from the tower, to make sure it was him.

RoseAnn cooked a great Italian meal for us that day, Guy was in his glory, and said, "We don't get food like this in here. Thanks Mom."

The second day, while walking on the path outside, I heard some guys talking. I walked over to look through the fence and I saw a bunch of inmates, some were exercising and playing ball and some just sitting around talking. Guy came over and said, "That's my coach on the ball team." He yelled through the fence and called the coach over. Guy introduced RoseAnn and me to the coach; he was a nice man who worked for the prison as a counselor as well as the baseball coach.

After a few minutes the coach said, "I shouldn't be doing this, you are on a family visit and contact with anyone else is not allowed."

I thanked him for talking to us and telling us how good a player Guy was.

With that, we walked back to the apartment, watched some black-and-white TV on a twenty-five-inch screen, and Ro cooked another great meal. We settled in and talked to Guy about his plans for the future. His plans all sounded good, but that would remain to be seen.

At 6:00 A.M. the following morning, our stay was over. We hugged Guy and left with tears in our eyes. We were there for two days, in prison just like everyone else, but we were getting out. He had another year to go. I don't think I could have stayed another hour without going berserk. How degrading!

It was very hard leaving him there and not being able to do a thing about it, after all this was our son, but he was in the system and had to do the time.

The next chapter brings a little more light as to what caused all of these problems.

43

Bipolar Disorder

Again I had to go to work. I had to go make people laugh while my son suffered from drug addiction. When he was released from prison, he came back to live with us. We wondered if he would use drugs again, would he be sent to jail again, or die from an overdose? Never knowing what was going to be, my wife had to stay home while I went back to comedy. Right—it was the only way I knew how to make a living. I was having fun, and my wife was suffering all the while. She didn't have the release I had. But when I finished work, we suffered together. Finally it got to the place where we both decided we'd had enough. We told him, "Guy, you're out. You're on your own. You're going to do what you're going to do. If this is the kind of life you are going to live, we're finished. We are through. We are done."

So he stopped using for a while. Then he couldn't understand what was happening to him and said his mind was going "wacky"—something was pushing him. We thought it was just an excuse. "What do you mean, pushing you? That's just your choice." So we talked to a couple of doctors, and after being analyzed and examined, we were told that he had bipolar disorder.

After reading books, hearing what the doctors had to say, and going to different meetings, we learned that people with bipolar disorder often self-medicated, to get the "wackiness" out. Their minds go in many different directions at once, which is very devastating. So they use drugs, alcohol—whatever they can find to make their minds settle down.

Even with all the doctors, the medications, the trial and error, not everything worked right away. He was on lithium for a while. That destroyed his thyroid, so even now he has to take medication for his thyroid condition. So until we found something that worked, life was very difficult—*very* difficult.

Now, on the right medications, he is doing very well. He's working, writing and editing films. It's one day at a time. That's how we take it, not knowing what tomorrow is going to bring. So we just sit and hope and pray that everything's going to be fine.

44

I'm a Grandpa, Thanks to Guy

There was a time when Guy went to California to break into the "big time." While he was there, pursuing a career and waiting for me to send him money (which he always needed), he started dating a beautiful young lady. She lived in Santa Ana, and Guy moved into a little apartment there to be near her. He brought her back to New York to visit—and lo and behold, she was pregnant. We'll call her Angela, for the sake of the book.

Naturally we were happy for both of them. They had a good visit and went back to Santa Ana. When Angela was in the eighth month of her pregnancy, she and Guy had a big falling out, and he returned home to stay with us.

The baby was born on April 18, 1997, and Angela named him Joseph. We tried to get in touch with her, to talk about our new grandchild, but she was so angry at Guy that she did not want any communication with us at all.

Finally, after trying for three years, I called and said, "I think we are entitled to see our grandchild." I was pretty insistent. "After all, Angela, it's the right thing to do. Meanwhile, please at least send us a picture."

So she sent a picture, and we were so thrilled to see this beautiful child, who looked just like Guy. We felt the door was now opened, so we made arrangements to go out to Santa Ana and meet Joseph. Guy was with us, but Ro and I decided to meet the boy alone the first time, to break the ice.

We had such a great day with him, laughing a lot, kissing, and hugging. We wanted to show him what we were all about, and he took to us right away. The next day we told Angela that it was time for him to meet his father, and she agreed. Guy was all nervous and anxious to see him.

We met them in a parking lot near a restaurant we were going to go to eat. Guy walked over to Joseph and said, "Hi—I'm your daddy and I love you." Well, Joseph looked at him with a strange glint in his eyes, not quite sure how to take it. After all, he was only three, but you could tell how smart he was. Meanwhile, Guy was sweating, not knowing how his son would respond to him. Well, by the end of the day he was calling Guy "Daddy," and how that filled our hearts with joy!

As of this writing, Joseph is thirteen, and he comes to Florida to stay with us in the summers. When I'm in California, we visit him, and Guy is always in contact with him. They love each other dearly, and over the years Angela has softened and we're all good friends. What a blessing!

45

Movies and Television

In 1990, while headlining at Resorts International in Atlantic City, I got a call from a casting agent in New York City. They were casting a movie called *Out for Justice,* with Steven Segal, and they wanted to see me the next morning. I told RoseAnn about it and said, "I've got to travel all the way up there to see them, and come back here and do a show tonight. I'm going to be a wreck." I'd have to get up at 7:00 to make the 10:30 audition.

She said, "Are you nuts? Just go. Things are starting to open up for you. Take advantage of it."

So I called a car service and asked if they would give me a special rate to drive to New York City for a day. They agreed, and I went to New York City for the audition. I arrived at the audition on time, and they asked if I could come back at 2:00 to meet with Steven Segal. I thought, *Oh, man—I'm going to have to go right on stage when I get back for the 8:00 show.* I said, "Okay, I'll do it."

At 2:00 that afternoon, I met Steven Segal for the audition. I read the script with him. When we were done, Steven asked what I was doing right now, and I said to myself, *He asked what I'm doing right now.* So I explained that I was doing a show in Atlantic City and I couldn't be waiting around there all day! They laughed, I laughed, and then I left.

I went back to Atlantic City and did my shows. After I finished, Ro and I went to an Italian restaurant for dinner, and the maître d' told me I had a call. It was Pamela Basker, who was casting the movie. "We would like to see you tomorrow at noon," she said.

I said to RoseAnn, "I got a call back. I have to go back to the city." Then I said to Pamela, "Listen, I'll come up, but are we close?"

"We're close," she said. "Warner Brothers will pay for you to come up." So I went.

I was closer than I thought I was. When I got to the meeting at the hotel, there was a room full of actors and agents. Steven Segal and Jules Nasso were in the room, and Steven looked at me and said he wanted to read from the script.

"What script?" I asked. "I don't have a script."

He said to his assistant, "Didn't I tell you when this guy left the room to give him a script for the role of Frankie? I told you when he left the room that we wanted him for the role of Frankie!"

"Nobody ever told me," I said.

"You are cast," he said.

"I am?" I asked incredulously. "Nobody told me. Thank you very much!"

Suddenly Steven and the producer approached me. They said they noticed that I had skin tags under my lower eyelids. They wanted to know if I would have them removed. I said, "Sure, but who's going to pay for this?" They said Warner Brothers would pay for it.

So I went to the plastic surgeon's office to have the skin tags removed, at Warner Brothers' expense. I went back to the production office a few days later, and they were very happy. They wanted me to look closer to Steven's age. I asked Steven how he liked it. He said, "Looks good."

I said, "How about we do the nose?"

He laughed, and the next thing I knew I was co-starring in the movie *Out for Justice*. I was very proud of it, and I figured I'd better listen to my wife from now on. She knows what's best for me.

After that, other offers came for movies and television, but my thing was comedy. I missed out on a lot of roles because I was out of town performing, and couldn't make auditions. Maybe I would have been a motion-picture actor today, or retired. In comedy, you don't retire. I'm still working and making people laugh. I guess that was God's plan for me.

46

What? I Have Cancer?

Remember earlier in the story when I told you I stopped drinking and smoking? Well, I did. In 1987, I stopped smoking and drinking, both cold turkey, and have never smoked or picked up a drink since. In 1991, I was on stage and I lost my voice while performing. I thought it was occupational, that I'd gotten laryngitis. I couldn't perform, so I hired somebody to fill in for me for the next night. I went to the doctor and had my throat checked. They put a tube through my nose and down my throat to see what was going on.

They called what I had leukoplakia—white patches that develop on the vocal chords, a pre-cancerous condition. They said that four out of a hundred people develop cancer from this. After more tests, they told me that I had cancer in my right vocal chord. Lucky me—I was one of the four out of a hundred. I said, "So doctor, what do we do now?"

He said they could try scraping it away, but if they took too much I would have a raspy voice the rest of my life.

I said, "No, no—that would be the end of my career. What other options are there?"

He said we could try cobalt radiation therapy—hopefully that would work.

So I proceeded to have thirty-six radiation therapy treatments. I continued working until I couldn't speak anymore. After thirty-six weeks of radiation treatments, my face got red and swelled up from the radiation and the medicine I was on. I was out of work for five months before I could speak clearly.

I was tested every two weeks, then three, then every month, and the cancer wasn't there. It was gone, but I was still having a little trouble with my throat. During the treatment, eating had been very difficult. Just one grain of rice felt like a boulder going down my throat, but I had to eat. I had to deal with the pain and do the best I could.

Finally I felt a little better, then better still, so I said, "Time to get back to work." So I did, but I was so frightened when I got on stage. *If I lose my voice while working, that's is going to be it. It's going to be over.* I said a prayer and asked Mom and Sal Junior to protect me while I was out there.

Well, my prayer was answered—I did it! The jokes, songs, I just blocked it out. It was like nothing was wrong with me. That was 1991, and the cancer never came back. So maybe God has another plan for me. Maybe he wants me here for a reason. Who knows? I just consider myself very lucky that I beat the cancer.

47

Quadruple Bypass

Some years later, in 2001, I started to feel tired all the time. (We were now living in Florida, but we kept an apartment in Lake Grove, Long Island, and that's where we happened to be at the time.) I was having trouble breathing from time to time, so I decided to go to the cardiologist to get an examination. He suggested I take a stress test, and after that test, he suggested an angiogram.

After the angiogram, I was in the recovery room when the doctor came in and told me that I had blocked arteries around my heart—90 percent blockage in three arteries. I needed open-heart surgery. He asked me when I wanted to do this.

"What do you mean, 'when'?" I asked.

"We can get you in Wednesday," he explained.

I said, "Hold it! I'm not coming in for a haircut. I have to think about it."

"If I were you," he said. "I wouldn't wait too long."

I said, "I need to check this out—interview some surgeons about the procedures, the charges."

So he gave me nitroglycerine to put under my tongue in case I had chest pains and told me to go to the emergency room if that happened.

So I started interviewing doctors at St. Francis Hospital until I found a doctor who would do something I'd heard about—the off-the-pump procedure, where they don't stop the heart and lungs from functioning while they do the bypass. It's a minimal access procedure, and that appealed to me.

Two doctors told me I wasn't a candidate for that procedure, but that was what I wanted to try. Then I found a Dr. La Mendola, who said I probably *was* a candidate for it, although he wouldn't know for sure until I was opened up on the table. But from what he could see, he felt the procedure would work for me—and sure enough, it did!

Afterward I learned that when he went into my body and got to my heart, they found that another artery at the back of my heart was a 100 percent blocked, so I wound up with a quadruple bypass. The end result—Dr. La Mendola was right. The surgery must have been a success, because I'm here to talk about it. That was eight years ago as of this writing, and I feel fine.

But, as always, I have to add some humor. When I asked the doctor what the recuperation time was, he said it could be six weeks, eight weeks, ten weeks, twelve weeks—it all depended on the individual. I told him to put me down for six weeks, but he said he couldn't guarantee that. I said, "Put me down for six weeks because six weeks from today I'm opening at the Sands Hotel in Atlantic City and I'm going to be there." Sure enough, after six weeks of recuperation, I opened up at the Sands. That was about a month after 9/11. I went and did the two shows.

I had one show Friday and one show Saturday. I was moving around on stage as I usually did, and I saw my wife in the audience, waving at me to slow down. But I just kept going. I felt fine; my adrenaline was going, and I was flying. But by the time I got into the limousine to go home, as soon as they shut the door, I almost collapsed into the seat. I was pale, and I fell into my wife's arms. I was almost in tears. It had finally caught up to me. I was wrecked. I slept all the way home, but then I rested two weeks before going to the cardiologist. Luckily, everything was fine. He said to keep doing what I had to do and to watch my diet and everything that went along with it.

48
Sal's Restaurant

Now it was 2004, and not knowing if I should continue to work as much as I had been, I decided to open a restaurant down in Florida. That's the one thing you should do after having quadruple bypass surgery, right? You should open a restaurant and work 24/7. So I opened the Sal Richards Supper Club, with music on weekends and a fabulous executive chef, Willy Figueroa. I got Guy in there, and he started to run the place as maître d.' I also got RoseAnn in there—but why not? It's a family-owned place.

All of a sudden I felt myself getting tired all the time again. I felt pain in the left side of my abdomen. It was a hernia, so now I had to have a hernia operation. I said, "What the hell am I doing to myself? Bullshit. This is going to stop. I'm going to take a vacation. That's it." So I sold the restaurant. It was nice, but I'd never do it again.

People were saddened by our closing, though. There was no place in the West Palm Beach area where they could go and listen to a live band and dance and have a great time until 1:00 in the morning. It would have been a great thing if I were younger. To own a restaurant at my age at that time was too much. No more restaurants for me. I would stick to comedy.

49
Ups and Downs

To say that my life resembled a roller coaster would be an understatement. As you've read so far, there have been ups and downs. Well, here are a few more.

Many years ago, I was up for a role on the *Rhoda* show, with Valerie Harper. It was between me and David Groh. It went right down to the wire and, okay—they picked David, but I was happy that they'd even considered me and I got that close.

Another time I went to California and was picked to do a television pilot called *Bachelor Life,* and I played one of the leads in the ensemble cast. We got ready to sign for twenty-two episodes, and that could have turned my whole career around. As it turned out, they decided to go with another show, called *Wild Flower,* which got canceled after three airings. They tried to get *Bachelor Life* back on, but it just wouldn't happen.

But there have been many rewarding experiences as well. Winning a few awards was among them—the kind of recognition that will always mean a lot to me.

In 1972, I won the award for Most Promising New Act in the Catskills by the Academy Of Variety Artists. A few years later, in 1975, I was named Entertainer of the Year by the same organization. It was an honor, to say the least. This, of course, happened before the ride got even rougher.

Then in 1997, I was inducted into the Celebrity Path in the Botanical Gardens in Brooklyn, and there was a big ceremony that day. I'm in great company too—among the others honored were Joe Torre, Cal Abrams (of the old Brooklyn Dodgers), singer Lainie Kazan, actor Tony Lo Bianco, and actors and writers Joe Bologna and Renée Taylor. We all have cement stepping-stones on the path with our names on it for eternity. It's not the Hollywood Walk of Fame, but if you're from Brooklyn, it means a lot.

This ceremony goes back many years, and it occurs on "Back to Brooklyn Day." Past inductees include Woody Allen, Barbra Streisand, Connie Stevens, Buddy Hackett, Jackie Gleason, the Ritz Brothers, and Jerry Stiller—just to name a few. They're all from Brooklyn, and what a thrill it was to be added to that list.

So maybe the ups and downs in my life have taught me a lesson— that I had to use my mind a little better, that I needed to sit down and analyze situations and make right decisions instead of making impulsive ones. I've always known that I had to do what was going to be right for me and my family. So now it's not ups and downs anymore. Now it's a question of working—getting booked and doing my show. Even at my age I'm still as vibrant and exciting on stage as I've always been. I believe I've even gotten better because I've learned a lot.

Being at home with my wife RoseAnn, and knowing my son, Guy, is doing better now, helps a lot. The pressures are going away. Will there be a time when I slow down? Maybe. Or maybe I will just keep going until they stop laughing. That's a joke. They won't stop, because if they do, that'll mean I died, REALLY!

50

The Future

I do have a couple of things in the works. I'm negotiating with a film distributor for a documentary that was done on my life. This was initiated by my cousin, Gregory Principato, whose late mother Annie and I were very close. She always asked me if I could help Gregory with his film career. Unfortunately I did not know anyone at the time who could help.

Back in 1996 I'd had a gig at the Trump Castle in Atlantic City, and Greg and I were talking about him bringing a crew to film my show. We'd make a DVD and try to sell it. By this time he had learned about filmmaking in college and working on television sitcoms.

We arrived at the Trump Castle on December 25, Christmas Day. While driving down to AC in the limo, the radio was on, and we heard that Dean Martin had passed away. I was upset, to say the least. I'd admired him all my life, and I'd had the pleasure of meeting him when I appeared in Vegas. He was a great person, one of the most respected acts in the business.

On December 26, opening night—ironically Sal Junior's birthday—the film crew set up, and we "shot the show." The next day, after viewing some of the footage, we both thought we might have something bigger than just a DVD to sell—we had the potential for a documentary. You see, he didn't just shoot the show—he covered the dressing room, checking into the hotel, the afternoon in our suite with friends, the limo ride, and the sign on the highway with my name as big as life.

A few months later, we decided a documentary was the way to go, so we formed a company—Laughing Angel Productions, which was named for his mother and our son.

Gregory and his crew followed me on and off for ten years, filming away, and finally after shooting eighty hours of footage and two years of editing, *Mr. Laughs: A Look Behind the Curtain* was finished.

We were able to get actor Vincent D'Onofrio, of *Law and Order—Criminal Intent* and many movies, to do the narration. Gregory was able to get him because he'd worked as a cameraman on the show and knew Vincent very well. When we had a screening at the Friars Club in New York, Vincent showed up and was very gracious with the people who came to see the movie. What a great guy!

We also asked some stars that I have known throughout the years to comment in the film—Don Rickles, Sid Caesar, Jackie Mason, Soupy Sales, Joy Behar, Julius LaRosa, Jerry Vale, Norm Crosby, Lainie Kazan, Freddie Roman, Johnny Dark, the late Red Buttons, the late Joe Viterelli (who played in *Analyze This*), and comic Jack Fontana. Also in the movie are my brother Steve, my sister Debbie, my late father, Steven Massaro Sr., and a dear friend who I have known for forty-five years, Jerry Cardone. He has a pivotal part in this film. We were kids together, and I was an usher at his wedding. He knows me better than anyone else in the movie, and he explains how he watched me grow.

In 2008 and 2009, *Mr. Laughs* won six best feature documentary awards at various film festivals around the United States. This book is like a companion to the movie, which can be purchased at Amazon.com. Usually it's the book first, then the movie, but we did it in reverse. So go buy the movie and have some fun.

Also as of this writing, I am getting ready to film a pilot for TV. It stars Lainie Kazan, Jerry Stiller, and Rene Taylor. I play Lainie's boyfriend. It is being directed by David Steinberg, and produced by Bonnie Bruckheimer. We will see what happens.

Epilogue

So now I've told my story. There is so much more, but I feel I have covered the things that were important in my life. If I don't stop writing now, this book would be the size of an encyclopedia. There were a lot of good times among the bad times—parties, family gatherings, birthdays, and so on. There were great times. But life is made of all the things I spoke about, so we have to be strong through it all and keep the faith. As you have read, it is a conglomerate of how to keep your sanity in times of trouble and to remain a human being.

There are probably hundreds of stories out there with some of the same situations, but not everybody handles them the same way. Hopefully this will encourage those who have suffered as we have to know that life goes on. We cannot change what is, and must unfortunately accept the hands we are dealt. But don't ever quit. Chase your dreams and—most importantly—keep the words "love, family, and God" in your vocabulary always.

GIVE SOMEONE A HUG TODAY!

LaVergne, TN USA
05 July 2010
188376LV00001B/94/P